SOFIA A. SOULI

The LOVE LIFE OF THE ANCIENT GREEKS

EDITIONS

TOUBI'S ®

ΕΚΔΟΣΕΙΣ

© Copyright 1997   MICHAEL TOUBIS PUBLICATIONS S.A.
                    Nisiza Karela, Koropi, Attiki.
                    Telephone: +30 210 6029974, Fax: +30 210 6646856
                    Web Site: http://www.toubis.gr

10-2001

ISBN: 960-540-224-6

Chronological Chart

The first European civilization develops on Crete:	3200 - 1200
The descent of the first Indoeuropeans into Greece:	3000 - 2000
The settliment of the first Greeks (propably Ionians) in continental Greece:	2000
The settlement of the Achaeans in Greece:	1750
Linear-A in Crete:	1570
Mycenean period. Settlement of the Achaeans in Crete:	1550 - 1200
Linear-B Schrift. Destruction of the paaces on Crete:	1450 - 1400
Descent of the Dorians into Greece First Greek colony on the coast of Asia Minor:	1200 - 1100
Homeric epics:	850
Two and one half centuries of superb lyric poetry (Sappho, Pindar, Kallinos, Mimnermos, Theognis etc.):	700 - 450
Solon's Laws:	594
Dissolution of the tyran with the assassination of the tyran Ipprchos by Armodios and Aristoyeitonas:	514
The founding of democracy in Athens:	510

500:	The beging of the 5th Century that was called the Golden Age. Philosophy, art and oratory reach their aims.
490:	Victory of the Athenians against the Persians at Marathon.
480:	Battle of Thermopylae.
480:	The overwhelming victory of the Greeks against the Persians in he naal battle of Salamis.
479:	Victory of the Greeks against the Persians at Plataies.
479:	Victory in the naval battle off Mycalis.
432 - 404:	Peloponisian War
408:	The meeting of the Socrates and Plato.
399:	The conviction of Socrates by the Athenian state.
370:	Thebes reaches its acme.
359 - 336:	Philipp II., the supermacy of Macedonia.
338:	The battle of Cheroneia.
336 - 323:	Alexander the Great, King of Macedonia and lord and master of all Greece.

*F*or many hundreds of years ancient Greece illuminated the civilizations which were part of its firmament like a dazzling star. From the sunset of the ancient world until the present there have been countless studies following in the footprints of this civilization and using the wealth of material those distant periods have bequeathed us. Art, poetry, oratory, philosophy, the sciences...

Turning our thoughts to the people whose life's work all that was, we find that our curiousity has been aroused by these people, which was the most cultured of its time, and which experienced each and every thing. Inevitably we arrive at a subject that has occupied quite a number of minds right up to the present, some superficially and others in more depth.

— How did the ancient Greeks conduct their private lives, how did they behave during their more private moments? It is not at all strange for one to ask oneself:

— Just how did that mighty figure, with shield and spear, that warrior of the Battle of Marathon, make love?

Undoubtedly you have all heard stories from time to time, told without the slightest shred of humor, about those days of old, and you have perhaps asked yourselves whether these stories, or others like them, bear the smallest grain of truth. In any case, why deny it, we all to one degree or another like to hear a spicy tale now and then. Since we have already made our way, if rather lightly, into the heart of quite a serious matter, what would you say if we now endeavored to shed a little light on those aspects of the ancient Greek world that are perhaps still unknown to most of us? Of course, we are dealing with a subject about which many writers have had a lot to say, or rather have glossed over, leaving a guilty silence. But the ancient Greek world has never had to ask for judges or censors. It has always shone forth, in the light of eternal spirituality! If we are to benefit from our endeavors then we must approach that society in a spirit of understanding which moreover is necessary if we are to view it without prejudice and enter into its process of thinking.

First of all we must clear up just what it is we mean when we say "antiquity". We cannot merely say that something happened in antiquity because we would be referring to a very large period of time, one which lasted for at least 1,200 years!

This means that the events that ran through this period that lasted for over a millennium brought about many changes in manners, customs, culture and traditions. Laws were enacted, laws were abolished, there were even changes in the map! Looking at the cities that one after the other flourished and then declined, we can all readily comprehend the influence that this must have had on the development of societies.

So the chronological framework of antiquity is a very large one, which is why we will only be referring to certain characteristic periods, such as Homeric times (8th century B.C.) and the centuries during which the major Greek city-states were at their peak (6th - 3rd century B.C.), which, in any case, have the most data to give us.

Another point that must be emphasized here is the influence that religion exercised during that period. Christianity, which imposed strict rules on personal, family and social life came much later. The ancient world with its polytheism, had a different view of life and other values. Not only did it not deem it necessary to cover the naked body but it deified this beauty through its incomparable art. The concept "καλός καγαθός" ("the character of nobleness") meaning that the virtue of the soul and the beauty of the body went hand in hand, was the basis of its creed.

Just the mere presence of Aphrodite in the pantheon, the goddess who represented sexual love and the joy of life, leads us to the realization that these people lived freely and confronted the reality of their own natures in a natural way. Nevertheless, in order to become fully reconciled to our subject, we have to accept that we are dealing with a different society, whose institutions and customs were radically different from our present-day moral perceptions. Thus, we will proceed with open eyes and seek to become acquainted with the spirituality of this society in order not to leave any room for exaggeration or odd personal interpretations which have been known to occur. Let us free ourselves then, if we can put it like that, from the bonds of our own social morality and let each of us put aside for a while his or her own feeling of what "ought to be". We are going to penetrate with a somewhat indiscreet eye into the ancient Greeks' personal affairs without forgetting that modern opinion means nothing to them. So let us approach the grandeur of virtue, as they conceived it. Any different way of looking at it, any different position taken, would do them a great injustice!

1

A FEW WORDS ON EROS

Hesiod - Homer - Sophocles - Lyric poets
The socratic Symposium
The meaning of Eros in platonic Philosophy

The little winged cherub with rosy cheeks holding a bow and cunningly shooting arrows, a figure taken straight from the inspiration of artists, is the image we have of Eros (the Greek god whom we in the West know as Cupid) that countless paintings, sculptures and other works of art have

"Erotes" decorating the handle of a vase (Munich painter)

her kingdom consists of the faithful who are the victims of strong passions and are permanently embroiled in a multitude of love affairs, lost in a sea of delight and not infrequently in a confused welter of problems. The allure of this goddess has spread through everything, from the Homeric epics down to the final

spread around the world. But just exactly who is this Eros from the ancient world? **Hesiod**, in his Theogony refers to him as being there at the very beginning of Creation: "First Chaos was born, the broad, stable and eternal earth and Eros..." This shows without a doubt that from mankind's very inception it was understood that eros [love and sex] directed and regulated the life and the happiness of human beings. The face of love is multi-dimensional and the interpretations vary, as we shall see as we go along. In mythology, Aphrodite (Venus) is the goddess of love and

poetic works and the tragedies of the period. Nevertheless, in the famous work by **Plato**, The Symposium, where **Socrates** is presented along with other fellow interlocutors discussing love, we find a characteristic differentiation of meanings. Two kinds of love are spoken of, which are represented by the common Aphrodite, or Pandimos as she is called, and the Heavenly Aphrodite. The former has to do with the satisfying of our fleshly desires while the latter aims at the good of the person who loves someone, that is, at his or her moral perfection.

*The god Pan endeavoring
to embrace the naked Aphrodite
who is threatening him with her sandal.
A smiling Eros between them,
(100 B.C., Athens, Archaeological Museum).*

Hesiod

One of the finest of the early poets of Greek antiquity who through his didactic epic brought to ancient consciousness different perceptions then what one finds in the Homeric epics. It is not known precisely when he lived. The ancients believed that he came before Homer. The latest speculations have put him between the 8th and the 7th century. He came from Askra, Boeotia and lived among farmers and impoverished nobility. He too must have roamed around as a bard like Homer because his work was esteemed outside the boundaries of Boeotia. His famous Theogony, which gives information about the beginning of the cosmos and the gods of the ancient Greeks, and the *"Book of Days"* which brought the persecuted to the forestage of the world are works which promoted the idea of a just reward for the human being who worked hard. In all his works, for he left behind many works of poetry, can be seen the close relationship of religion to morality.

Sophocles

One of the three great tragedians of the 5th century B.C. (496 - 406). (Sophocles, Aeschylus and Euripides made up the great triad of tragedians who were the forerunners of the modern theater). He lived in Athens when it was at its cultural peak and his talent which appears so clearly in his work attracted the interest and the admiration of his contemporaries. He was a close friend of Herodotus. This superb dramatist and crafter of language left behind an important body of work. Some of his famous plays are "Ajax", "Antigone", "Oedipus Tyrannos", "Electra" and "Philoctetes".

Before getting into an analysis of this subject, which is the key to a whole philosophy, let us take a quick look at the first part, the more common and everyday one. Eros, as we understand it today, was honored in the ancient world and exalted more than anything else. The tragedian **Sophocles**, in his famous play Antigone, has left us the well-known song of the Chorus:

> *Love invincible*
> *you who keep vigil*
> *on maidens' cheeks*
> *you who conquer those you draw near*
> *rich or poor*
> *you even traverse the sea*
> *and not one of the immortals*
> *has ever saved himself from you*
> *nor has any mortal escaped you*
> *in this graceless bitter life*
> *Sweet-smelling flower*
> *next to you reason and reflection*
> *flee in flight.*

A breathtaking lyricism dominates all the works of the ancient Greek poets when they are praising love.

Beautiful Helen of Troy with Paris (Nadar).

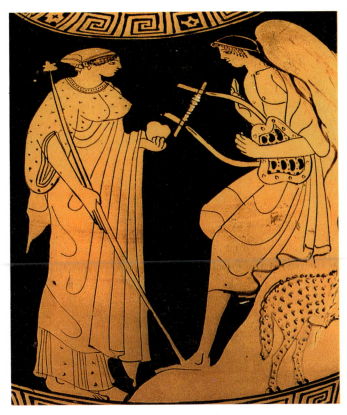

Hera giving the apple
to Paris who appears consternated
(red-figured hydria, 480-460 B.C.,
London British Museum).

In mythology the loves, marriages and repeated couplings of the gods, Zeus and Poseidon in particular, produced generations of demigod heroes, who were then enlisted in the struggle for good.

Homer's epics are infused with an atmosphere of "poetic eroticism", it would be fair to say. The goddess Aphrodite's promise of a life of love-making with the most beautiful woman in the world was the bait laid for Paris, who in the end offers her the apple of discord. The love of Paris for Menelaos' exquisitely beautiful Helen set the stage for the greatest war in antiquity. For ten years the Achaeans lay siege to Troy in order to take back Helen, whose relationship to Eros had become both an idea and a symbol.

These myths continued to serve as points of reference for human beings in historical times, from the eighth century B.C. on, and constituted the historical truth of their time. The ancient eras succeeded one another and the Greeks experienced love through the customs and the institutional framework of each period.

Homer

Homer is the greatest poet of all time. He lived in the 9th century B.C. and few facts are known about his life, nor are we even sure where he was born, though seven towns of antiquity have claimed the honor: Smyrna, Rhodes, Colophon, Salamis on Cyprus, Chios, Argos and Athens. The most likely is Smyrna because his work contains many Ionian elements. His immortal epics The *Iliad* and The *Odyssey* are the most ancient and the most remarkable literary works we have in our possession while many other works are also attributed to him.

Love paralyzes my limbs.
Again this serpent upsets me,
sweet, bitter, motionless.

Sappho

Boy bring wine,
bring water and then
the flower-entwined wreathes
come put them on me
so I may begin to spar
with Eros again.

Anacreon

Savage love has pierced and
bound my heart
my eyes have dimmed
and even the peace of my soul
is stolen from my breast.

Archilochos

All we have learned is based on evaluations that have been made by various authorities since then and can in no way be considered as absolute. An entire world appears before our eyes through the pottery, drawings, statues and various pieces of sculpture, whose representations all serve us as data. In combination with these, the texts that have survived from the same periods shed sufficient light on the subject we wish to discuss. But whatever way we look at it, artistic depictions can only characterize their period to a certain point and primarily because all we have at our disposal is what has survived. If we then add to this what foreign artists have left behind, from their journeys through one place and another, all the influences that were at work and even the objectives that were served by these depictions, we will be led to the conclusion that this is not such a simple matter. For example, during the fourth century when expression in art was so free, it is known that artists did not represent only scenes from daily life in their works but also their own personal inclinations, stresses and uneasiness, and not infrequently they took a satirical attitude toward things, as can be seen in some of the representations which contain exaggerations. But let us not get overly involved with that. Conversations on love appear to have certain elements which stay the same down through time.

Scene from an orgy with hetairas.

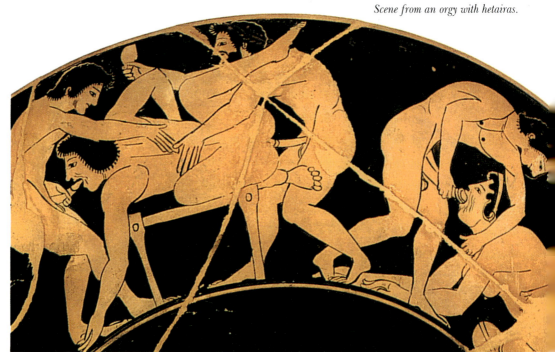

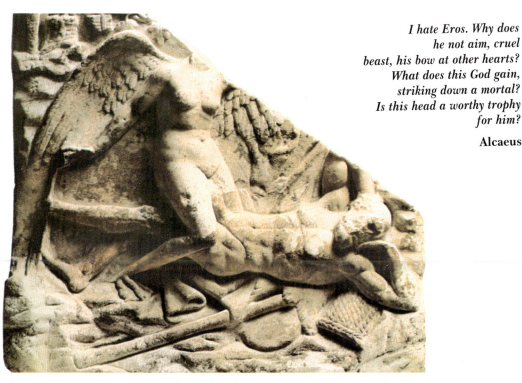

The meaning of eros in platonic philosophy

*L*et us turn to the second part of our investigation of love, Heavenly Aphrodite as she was referred to by Plato. This is the concept of love that the great philosopher Socrates was most concerned with, because Eros as the most ancient of the gods was also thought to be the most important for the securing of virtue and happiness, not only in this life but in the one that came after it as well. This form of eros had a very high aim indeed!

Our next thought is as follows: just how can this "magical" element in eros be made to function with the aim of achieving virtue? We have reached the point where we have to clarify the concept of "eros" in somewhat more detail. There are difficulties involved with the present-day Greek language because the words "love, passion and the sexual act", "lover" "someone in love, sweetheart" and "to be in love, to fall in love" all have slightly different interpretations. The ancient verb "ερώ" did not mean either "I love" nor "I am in love" in the modern sense. The verb for that kind of love, or eros, had a dynamic character. When the Greek of that period said "ερώ" he meant "I long for, I yearn", that is, "I am continually seeking through my soul for whatever I am lacking". A psychic need was contained within this verb, which sought a deeper satisfaction. Let us look at the difference.

Scene of lovemaking between a farmer and a Siren. Part of a marble offering (Boston, Museum of Fine Arts).

Like a fierce wind, Love shook my heart.

Sappho

Love, the ruler of the gods torments humans.

Anacreon

Bitter, sweet, insatiable and yet cruel it is the love of youth at full strength

Theognis

Plato

Plato was the second of the triad of ancient Greek philosophers (Socrates - Plato - Aristotle) who were the founders of the philosophy of western civilization. He was born in Athens, or on the island of Aegina, around 428-427 B.C., a year after the death of the great Pericles, and he died in 347-348 B.C. It is said that his original name was Aristoclis but since he had a broad forehead and chest ("platys") his contemporaries began to call him Plato during his adolescence. As a youth he was educated like the other youths of his time, while as a student of Socrates he became so attached to his philosophy that all his inclination toward poetry was transformed into philosophy. After the death of his teacher, Socrates, Plato left Athens and travelled in the Greek areas to the west, and even after his return to Athens he continued to play a part in the politics of Syracuse. He founded his own philosophical school, the Academy, in which the most noteworthy young men of the period studied and left behind many written works, transferring to us in this way the work of the great Socrates, who is always at the epicenter in all of Plato's writings.

I love my friend means that this relationship satisfies me. "Ερώ", however, means that I feel a love for wisdom, for valor, values that I never give up searching for, because I am a "lover" (admirer, worshipper) of wisdom and valor! So let us try and follow the thought of the Greek people and experience the miracle of a period that was destined to be called the Golden Age:

Eros in Platonic philosophy functions as a natural phenomenon. It turns toward the beautiful, as the sunflower turns toward the sun. We cannot identify eros solely with the reproductive instinct, no matter how closely connected it appears to be, because that instinct, as expressed through a physical act, refers to the process involved in a bodily function and this act can occur without any of the deeper meanings of the word "love".

Sensual or carnal pleasure ("ηδονή") is again not the purpose of true "eros" because it can never fulfill us as individuals, and because we gain it by exploiting in some way the beloved person who is thus diminished in this manner.

Physical love is destined by nature to lead to birth and to the perpetuation of the species. But the human being is a privileged being and differs from the rest of the creatures in creation because his intellect insures him a continuity in his life.

Aphrodite advising Cupid on where to aim. Mirror from the 4th century B.C.

Opposite page: The kiss. A scene from a Corinthian red-figured vase from the 6th century B.C. depicting a couple just about to kiss (Berlin, Archaeological Museum).

Socrates

He was the greatest philosopher to grace the Golden Age. He was born in Athens in 470 or 469 B.C. and he died there in 399 B.C. His powerful personality created around him a circle of friends and students who followed him with love and dedication but he also created enemies which led to his condemnation and death. His attitude during his unjust trial was characteristic because while he could have got himself off, he was steadfastly faithful to what he taught, that is, that one must obey the law. Greek philosophy was brought to full flower through his work as he redefined fundamental concepts of human life and the functions of the republic. He left no written work but his personality and his intellect were saved by the work of many of his contemporaries, above all Plato, who was a student and admirer as well as the one who carried on his work.

But we will not neglect the part eros plays in what is aesthetically beautiful. The beautiful and well-trained body was something that called forth admiration. And if the beauty of the body was of less importance than the beauty of the soul, it was still what constituted the indispensable basis for the ideal and was what originally attracted one. What was sought was a combination of somatic and psychic beauty. It is more difficult of course to find that faultless inner world of wisdom and virtue. These elements of somatic and psychic beauty are what serve to "erotically" connect two charismatic individuals. The ideal communication of these two individuals leads to the genesis of spiritual good. All these functions which are related to the flesh and its beauty and which create pleasurable feelings, have to do with the external world toward which this energy flows, but without losing any of its natural purity. The needs of the flesh are now of the second degree and their satisfaction aims at their liberation from problems inherent in life, so that no longer distracted by them people can apply themselves to great works.

Socrates considered this purity an inviolable condition for the maintenance of spiritual freedom and while he gives physical love a special place, he condemns it if it becomes a passion of the flesh because then the logical basis of the soul is lost and along with it its freedom.

So the conclusion we arrive at after all this is that eros in antiquity could mean carnal intercourse and all things related to it, but the word and its derivatives did not always operate solely in this sense. So there could be "eros" without any form of bodily contact. That is because the human being is considered to be a mortal, individual existence who participates in life by means of eros with the aim of both maintaining it and giving it the dimensions of immortality. Which is what ancient eros was to the Greek: *the longing for immortality!*

The Venus de Milo (Louvre).

Marble sculpture of Theseus with Antiope from the temple of Apollo at Eretria (500-490 B.C. Archaeological Museum of Eretria).

HE & SHE ... IN OLDER TIMES

The love-making of the Gods - Famous erotic myths
The woman in classical antiquity

The age old game of love between male and female is not only a phenomenon that has been continually repeated since time immemorial but is deterministic by its very nature. The care taken by nature to perpetuate the species shows it has put its diachronic seal of approval on it. In following these commands the man and woman of the ancient world found that the course of their passion intersected with feelings of love, reciprocity and creation without there being any lack, of course, of certain pernicious emotions. Let us turn our attention for a while to the psychic and somatic relationship that connects couples in terms of their era and their social context. Right from the very beginning, after the dissolution of the matriarchal societies and the concentration of authority in what we now call the powerful sex, the Greek people imagined their male gods as being hyperactive and immoderate virtuosos in an ongoing game of love with the beautiful sex, so that their male-dominated society would feel justified about its actions which were

Couple dressed in wedding attire

attributed to their gods. And let's start off with the father of the immortal gods himself, Zeus, who no sooner put his relationship with Hera on a legal basis, after his installation on Mt. Olympus, than he began to waltz around the may pole with all kinds of goddesses and female mortals. Who should we remember first? Maia who gave birth to the god Hermes as the fruit of their love-making, Semeli who gave him Dionysos, Leto, who despite Hera's jealousy managed to bring Apollo and Artemis into the world, Themis or Mnemosyni? It is worth noting that wherever there was a single girl blessed with fertility we can be sure that some god would have his way with her! Outside marriage? Abandoned? No, never! Here we are speaking of the divine seed, supernatural powers, heroes! There was general respect for the children of the immortal gods. So much divine cunning was needed to come up with the clever designs for the seduction of these ravishingly beautiful mortal women. Zeus transformed himself into a exquisite swan to get close to Leda, the mother of Castor and Polydeuces.

Leda and the swan. Mosaic from a Roman house in ancient Paphos on Cyprus.

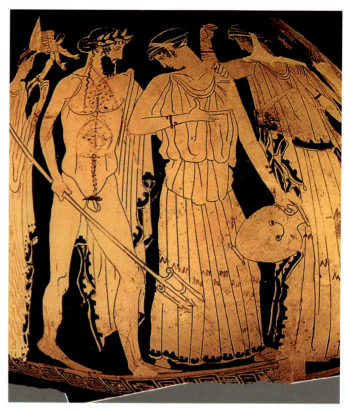

Erotically besieged by Poseidon the bashful Danaid Amymone tries to get away from him (red-figured pelike, 450 B.C., Rome Villa Giulia).

Another time the Olympian became a shower of gold in order to slip through the crack in the cave where Danae was locked up, and she gave birth to Perseus. And he appeared as a bull to first turn the head of and then abduct Europa!

As if it were only Zeus! There was Poseidon too; god of the sea, who despite his marriage to Amphitrite, was always... stirring up the waters.

In his unique way Homer in The Odyssey relates how Poseidon took the form of the river Enipeas in order to seduce Tyro who frequented its banks:

"...Resembling him who makes the earth shake and girds it,
he drew near to her at the foam-flecked mouth of the river
and lay down; a dark wave surrounded them like a mountain,
a bower over them, to hide the god and mortal woman.
There the god loosened the girdle of her virginity and
lulled her, and when he had finished the work of love
sweetly squeezed her hand and called to her and said:
"Rejoice that I embraced you; when time has passed
you will have lovely children, the love of the gods
does no one harm; care for our children and nurse them sweetly.
Go now be in peace and not a word;
but know that I am Poseidon and make the earth tremble...

The rest of the gods too were enamoured of chasing after love, no matter what element they happened to rule. Apollo may have been the god of light and pursued Daphne but one should not forget there is also the case of Pluto, the god of Hades, the underworld, who kidnapped Persephone to make her his companion in his sunless kingdom. And we will not even mention Aphrodite's carryings on since she was, after all, the goddess of love. But think of Pan that god with the ugly puss and goats' feet who was always running after some nymph. He even managed to seduce the enchanting and hard-to-please Selene with his wiles. And what about that non-stop party-animal Dionysos and his ever-present scandalous entourage, all of them in spectacular high spirits, singing, dancing and conducting orgies under the influence of plentiful wine!

I toss you an apple;
if you accept it
it means you love me
grant me your virginity
my girl.
But if you are of another mind
again accept the apple
so it may teach
you how ephemeral
is the beauty of love.

Plato

Famous erotic myths

But let us leave the gods aside since they could more or less take care of themselves. It is obvious that the period of antiquity when the love of man and woman flourished in both the psychic and somatic dimensions was the one that started during the time of Homer and lasted up until the pre-classical period.

Small statue of the god Pan sitting on a rock (Hellenistic period, Athens, Archaeological Museum).

23

*My dear mother I cannot
weave at the loom
Aphrodite has bound me with
a young man's passion.*

Sapphc

*Justice must be on the side
of those in love.*

Anacreon

*Young couple
about to make love
(430-420 B.C.).*

Mimnermos

A Greek elegiac poet from Colophon, Ionia who was active in the second half of the 7th century B.C. He is thought to be earlier than or contemporary with the Seven Wise Men of Ancient Greece and it is said that he knew Solon. He was the father of the love elegy and his poetry expresses deep emotions. Through his lines run a light strain of melancholy for the joys and sensual pleasures of youth that pass so quickly, and a fear of old age.
Mimnermos is distinguished as a great technician of the Greek language and the elegiac meter and is included in the ancient canon of elegiac poets.

Meleager

Meleager came from Gadara in Palestine. He lived around 100 B.C. and learned Greek in the schools of Tyre. Later he became a student of the philosopher Menippos. He died on the island of Kos at a great age. He wrote numerous epigrams, many to do with love, of which 134 have survived. His verses are lyrical and tender but realistic as well.

The flowers of youth are
seized by men
and women.

Mimnermos

The Three Graces decorated
and triple wreathed
the bed of Zenophilia so she
would have as her adornment
the awakening of the passion
of love, the brilliance of
beauty
and third and best of all the
word that enchants.

Meleager

Hermes, Orpheus and Eurydice
from the sculptures at the Athenian Agora, 5th century B.C.

Women in those days had considerably more freedom to move around in the cities so that they became living stimuli for the verses of the poets and the objects of erotic passion for the male population.

The love of Helen, the beautiful queen of Sparta, to which we referred in the preceding chapter, set its mark on a whole period. The faith that Penelope had in Odysseas and her dedication to him is something that transcends the values of the age. It is the projection of a moral force with has always been a blessing when it unite couples. Even in the Platonic "Symposium", in a period when the relationships between man and woman had undergone a change, there was a clear recognition of the rare and powerful love of Alcestis, the wife of Admittos, who wanted to die in his place when death came to take her husband. Conversely, the love of Orpheus was considered to be less powerful, because when he lost Eurydice, he did not choose to die for love but tried in every way possible to go down to Hades alive.

However, as one always finds, there was not only the prolific, fecundating love and the spiritually higher one. In line with human character and its passions, there was also the destructive passion which obliterated all in its mania of revenge.

The example of Phaedra, the wife of Theseus, is typical: in love with Hippolyte, the son of her husband, and not getting any response to her overtures, she condemned him forthwith, betraying him to his father in a most horrible manner, urging Theseus to seek the death of his own child! There is also the case of Medea who upon losing Jason did not hesitate for a moment to kill her own children to take her revenge on him. The ancient tragedies are full of incidents which sometimes praise the grandeur of love which reaches to the heights of the heavens themselves while at other times things come to a fateful and tragic conclusion. But one way or the other, this love, the "eros" between the two sexes, either as a way of confrontation and showdown, or a way of coexistence, was never missing.

The woman in classical antiquity

But let us go to the classical period, a period when society was male-dominated. The social system of the period proscribed the activities of women to a great degree. In fourth century Athens she did not receive the education and cultivation of the man, while any similar interests which would have given males and females the chance to be together were kept to a bare minimum, if not totally non-existent. Thus love in a psychic dimension, in the sense we mentioned in the preceding chapter, did not flourish with any ease, which is why "erotic" discourse was limited, in most instances, to a carnal level. The hetairas (rather like courtesans, mistresses and geishas all combined), whom we will speak of below, took care to acquire education so that they could be present at the gatherings of men. But only these females were allowed any freedom of movement during that period.

This does not mean of course that there were no loving couples in Athens, in the full sense of that phrase. Moreover, there was no period in which the woman resigned from her eternal role, her constant endeavor to attract the male.

Statue of an Athenian girl from the end of the Archaic period.

Women decorating the house with flowers for the wedding ceremony.

27

Plutarch

Plutarch was born in Chaironeia, Boeotia, and lived sometime in the period between 45 B.C. to 120 A.D. He was the last of the great Greek writers of antiquity. He was an important intellectual, influenced by Plato, and was involved with biographies, research into religion, ethics, psychology and pedagogical matters. He was educated in Athens and it appears that he was also trained in rhetoric. He made many trips and had particularly noteworthy contacts with the Delphians since he had the lifelong office of high priest and supervisor of the oracle. He is thought of as a prolific writer. His *"Ethics"* contains more than 78 works while his *"Lives"* is a panorama of ancient life, describing the life of eminent figures of Greek antiquity and comparing them to the lives of illustrious Romans. In this work he is concerned with twenty-four men and their counterparts in Rome. His writings are noted for their uplifting qualities, with examples to emulate, and always promoted what was most noble in life.

And while during the Archaic period, when she enjoyed his interest, we find that she frequently has her hair dressed in the same way as the man, we equally find that in a more difficult period, the classical, she went on the counterattack. The Athenian woman of that time arranged her hair in beautiful curls which she fixed high up at the back of her head. The younger ones tied their hair back with ribbons leaving the forehead free.

So in the struggle to increase her charm, the woman mobilized a host of weapons of female glamor: she used a cosmetic made of lead carbonate to make her skin whiter, and rouge from the root of the achousa plant, as Hesiod casually mentions when in one of his moods where he wished to bring her little secrets into the open. She used make-up on her eyes and eyelashes, she used depilatories, if you please, and her attire did not lack that female article par excellence the "breast-band", in other words a brassiere! All this beautification had but one aim: to make her more attractive in the eyes of men. Clothes, and jew-ellery, were also far from insignificant: ear-rings, rings, necklaces, and bracelets ornamented the woman of that far off period, quite a number of examples of which have come down to the present. But while Athenian fashion sought to keep garments sufficiently modest with long tunics and veils which wound around the body in beauti-ful folds at the proper points, in the tasteful manner we see

Relief from the frieze of the Parthenon showing the young Atthides who wove the veil (peplos) of the goddess Athena coming to dedicate it to her in honor of the Panathenaic Festival.

in statues, the opposite was true of Sparta where the young women wore short tunics or a veil secured in the middle, but unstitched at the side leaving the legs uncovered. This despite the more general severity of Laconian laws, perhaps because the girls were included in the educational system with the boys, on the banks of the Evrotas river, and such clothing made it easier to move. Thus the Spartan tunic, with a great deal of ease, left the thighs uncovered with the slightest movement, which provoked the caustic critique of the Athenians who mockingly referred to them as "thigh-revealers".

Plutarch believed that **Lycourgos**, the law-giver of Sparta, had his reasons for all that. The boys of Sparta would not have remained unmoved by their view of the half-naked girls and would thus have been inclined toward marriage. So marriage was the aim, the only institution in whose embrace, down through time, could the family, that cell essential to every society, develop.

Lycourgos

Spartan law-giver, creator of the political and social institutions of ancient Sparta who is thought to have lived around 780-750 B.C. Lycourgos made many trips in the Aegean, to Ionia and to Crete where he studied the political life of these areas. The Great Ritra, the political regime, that is, of Sparta, with the dual hereditary monarchy, the Senate and the convocation of the army which represented the people, was given to Lycourgos by the Delphic Oracle.
To the same person is attributed the strict reformation for the ownership of land and the sum total of laws which are related to the rules of life for the Spartans and the education of the young.

Couple in wedding attire adorn an ancient cup.

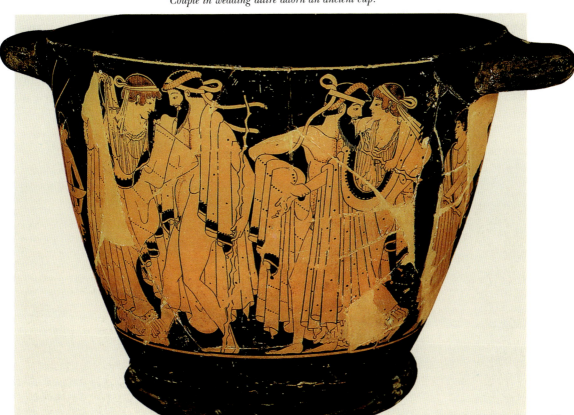

MARRIAGE... MOST ANCIENT

Marriage in mythical times - Marriage in historical times
The marriage ceremony - Marriage in Sparta

*I*t does not take any particularly laborious research to ascertain that from the start of the world the institution of marriage has passed from one society to another, in different forms perhaps but always powerful! In all states, even the most liberal ones, marriages are not only not limited, but on the contrary the institution always constitutes a positive social value because through it mankind reproduces itself. In Greek mythology we find that Zeus, after the establishment of his authority on Olympus, hastened to legitimize his relationship with Hera through marriage, and this always remained in force despite conjugal ups and downs. This shows the position and the importance that marriage had in the conscience of our distant ancestors. In the centuries-old history of the Greek people, the relationship between spouses and the rights of the female part of this relationship, have been directly connected to the position that woman held in each society. During the Homeric period women freely appeared in public places.

The marriage of Zeus and Hera (vase by Euphronios).

Trojan women moved about the city while Helen even circulated throughout the castle where the warriors were. During the Minoan period something similar held sway and perhaps even more advanced: we have bare-breasted women taking part in bull-leaping, in the contests with the bulls. In a scene from "The Odyssey", on the island of the Phaeaceans, the young daughter of the king, Nausicaa, goes down to the beach with her servants where she plays, bathes and amuses herself out in the open. All of this is related to what the established practices for marriage were during each period. So we see that during Homeric times marriage consisted of the abduction of or purchase of the woman. In several instances the father of the perspective bride organized a competition among the perspective suitors or set himself against them, such as in the case of Oinomaos, the father of Hippodameia, with his son-in-law to be Pelops, where the marriage took place after the triumph of the latter in a chariot race.

Odysseus and Penelope at the moment of their meeting. (Relief from Milos from 460-450 B.C., the Louvre).

The etiquette of that period called for the groom to offer the father of the bride, after the finalizing of the wedding agreement, the "edna", which were symbolic gifts or gifts of value, and to receive from his father-in-law the "meilia", which we can consider as a distant ancestor of the institution of the dowry. Then the bride put the palm of her hand in the man's palm and from that moment on they were considered man and wife. This was followed by a festive ceremony, the moving of the bride to her husband's home. What is worthy of note from that period is the position that the wife had in regard to her husband. The "lawful, wedded wife" of Homer was not only respected but also desirable and very much loved. Hector and Andromache, Odysseus and Penelope, Alkinoos and Arete are just a few of the many couples we could mention.

Marriage in mythical times

During historical times things were very different. The rights of the woman were much more restricted because she herself was completely subject to the man, the master of the house. The high point of antiquity, during the time of Pericles, found her with almost no privileges. She was forbidden to go out and circulate in the streets except on rare occasions. Only the very poor women, who were obliged to work in the market if they had no relative to support them, went into public places. Of course in the house the wife was still mistress of the slaves and directed the operation of the household but only when she had the confidence of her husband and was granted the authority by him, and he always retained the right to revoke that authority.

Marriage in classical Greece was conducted in two ways: with the "εγγύηση" ("pledge" or "guarantee") or through "επιδικασά" (the adjudgement of property). Under the first method, the guarantor, the master of the girl (father or guardian) handed over the bride, in front of witnesses, to the groom by means of a marriage contract and the amount that would be given as a dowry was then set. From what we understand of antiquity, even though they called marriage sacred, there was no kind of religious ceremony whatsoever. Nevertheless, the handing over of the dowry was what separated marriage from concubinage, that is the keeping of a woman in a man's house without marriage.

For a man there is nothing in the world better than a good woman or worse than a bad.

Simonides - Keios

Simonides - Keios

He was born on the island of Kea in the Cyclades in 556 B.C. and died in Acraganada Sicily in around 468. He was involved with all kinds of poetry but achieved lasting fame for his famous epigrams which are characterized by their elegant style, Doric spareness and poetic exaltation.

The institution of the guarantee held sway throughout nearly all ancient Greece. For the marriage to take place there was no need of consent on the woman's part.

The other method we mentioned, that of adjudgement, was applied when a girl was "an heiress" that is, when she had inherited the property from her father and there were no male heirs. The heiress had to marry one of the nearest descendant relatives so that the property would stay in the family. Those who were interested declared their intentions and everything then followed in line with a legal process according to which the nearest relative was the one who prevailed. It is self-evident that the motive for this kind of marriage was economic bene...

*My groom with what more
beautiful thing
may I compare you?
In my eyes you look just
like a graceful branch!*

Sappho

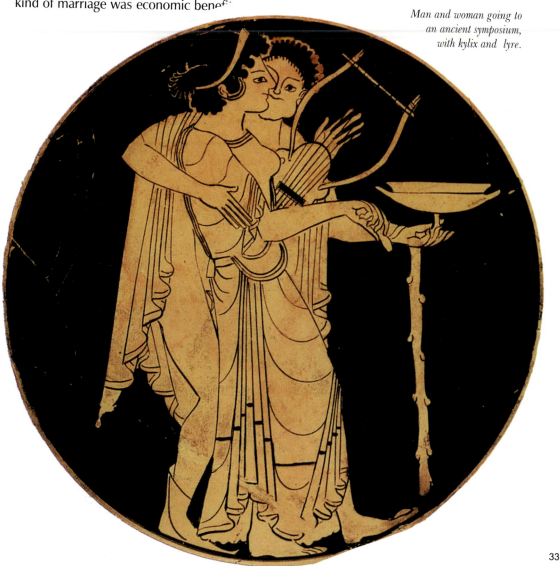

*Man and woman going to
an ancient symposium,
with kylix and lyre.*

Solon

He was an important politician and law-giver of ancient Athens, one of the Seven Wise Men of ancient Greece. He was born in 640 B.C. and died in approximately 560 B.C. Through his legislation he brought a halt to the exclusive state rule of the nobility (oligarchs) and put into application a merit system ("timocracy"). He established new humanistic laws, and in addition he was a noteworthy poet. Before he was elected legislator he travelled a great deal. At the beginning of the 6th century B.C. there was grinding poverty in Athens, the farmers did not have the money to pay the nobles, they lost their land and not infrequently became slaves. Solon invalidated all confiscation of land and liberated all citizens who had been forced into slavery. He forbade loans that used the individual liberty of the citizen as a guarantee and organized the commercial life of the region with the export of products and the minting of coins. With the new social division, the economically less powerful took part in social affairs. Solon was a moderate and condemned all extremes. He foresaw the laws he passed as staying in force for one hundred years. He himself travelled so they would not demand elucidations or changes from him that would be just for some but unjust for others.

Solon, however, drew up legislation that called for the man who took the heiress to have sexual contact with her, at least three times a month, so that a male child would be born as soon as possible. The law did not forbid incest. Only marriage between brothers and sisters who had the same mother was forbidden. Children of the same father, adopted siblings and cousins, could be married. Sinful incest was sexual relations between ascending and descending lines, such as in the case of **Oedipus** as seen in the play by Sophocles. This was a social and religious prohibition, the violation of which, it was believed, called down the rage and the just punishment of the gods. But in general, sexual relations between men and women and all forms of bodily contact were not condemned by religion nor were there any religious laws which imposed abstinence or purification. The same was true for the natural function of the woman, the one related to her fertility. All that was forbidden a couple was to make love in the sanctuary of a god.

As we proceed, it must be stressed that the selection of a husband was purely up to the guardian of each young woman. And since usually it was the father who had the final say, Herodotus mentions as an event worthy of note

Oedipus solves the riddle of the Sphinx (interior of a red-figured kylix, 470-460 B.C. Rome, the Vatican Museum).

the fact that a certain Athenian, when his three daughters had reached marriageable age, allowed them to choose among the likely suitors and married them to those that they chose. It appears therefore that in each period there were sensitive parents with "progressive" views and the example given by **Herodotus** could not have been the only case. Nevertheless, it is clear that love did not play any role in the matter. The free citizen had the right to seek sexual satisfaction with the hetairas and to have a concubine if he so wished. On the other hand, discussion and mingling of intellectual interests with the spouse were non-existent because women had not acquired any education. So just what purpose did marriage serve? But we already said what that was at the beginning: the purpose was to pro-duce children.

It was of prime importance to them, as part of their duty as citizens, to leave behind legitimate male descendants. For that reason there were regulations that provided for this which were drawn up by the law-givers, both by Solon in Athens and Lycourgos in Sparta.

Looked at from an ethical point of view, a couple demonstrated through marriage their desire to leave some-one behind who would take care of their funeral. Those who did not produce male descendants adopted a boy for that purpose. Another motive for marriage had to do with economics, because frequently the dowry was quite a sig-nificant amount, so much so that a man would often not divorce a woman because if he did his family would have to return it.

The attributes of what made up a true marriage during that period, become completely clear when reading the advice that Hesiod gave to men. In this matter, **Hesiod** counselled that a man ought to bring a woman into his home before he was over the age of thirty, and he judged the best age for the female partner to be 15 or 16. He also recommended that she be a respectful virgin and above all else that she came from a related, or at least friendly fam-ily, so she would know the customs of the house she would be living in. He stressed that a good wife is the greatest possession, while conversely a bad wife becomes the cause for a great deal of harm. And he ended by advis-ing that one avoid women of spirit who have a swing to their step and are coquettish because they will surely neglect their household duties.

Herodotus

The earliest Greek historian, who for that reason was called the "father of history" by Cicero. He was born in Halicarnassus in Asia Minor around 480 B.C. and died in 420 B.C. He came to Athens before 445 B.C.where he wrote about the eminent figures of the time and was honored by the Athenian State and Pericles with a significant amount of money for his texts. Later he settled in Thourios, a panhellenic colony in Magna Grecia (Lower Italy) where he also died. His historical work is quite substantial. He recounted the Medean Wars, Persian expansionism, the Greek-Persian Wars and many details concerning the life of the Egyptians, the Scythians and other nations. He wrote in a noble style, stressing the beautiful and the elevated, and combining an interest in anthropology, ethnology, ethnography, naturalism and sociology, but he took more of an overview than he should have on details and it is thought that there are imprecisions and exaggerations in his statistical data.

Pericles

He was born in Athens in 495 B.C. and died in 429 B.C. He was the leader of the Athenian Democracy for more than thirty years. After the definitive defeat of the Persians he began his activity in the political arena. He succeeded in founding and developing democracy in Athens and at the same time to develop it into a naval empire and the dominant force in Greece during the second half of the 5th century B.C. To Pericles' program of action are owed most of the classical monuments of antiquity and of course the famous Acropolis. So this period is rightly called the "Golden Age of Pericles". His personality was so powerful that within a democratic regime with many political opponents, his ability was recognized to the point that he held concentrated in himself the greatest power of any politician in antiquity.

Aspasia

She was born in Miletos and came to Athens as a hetaira in 455 B.C. at the age of 20. Her beauty, her education, her intelligence and her eloquence immediately set her apart in a world that was very hard on the women of that period. She came into contact with all the noteworthy men and after she became acquainted with Pericles he immediately separated from his first wife and began to live with Aspasia. She taught him a great deal and inspired him with visions and words which he proclaimed with success. Their house was transformed into a meeting-place for the wise men of the time, and orators and artists and the incredible intellectual activity of Athens came to full flower there. After her union with Pericles she gave birth to a son who was made legitimate much later with a law passed in 430 B.C.

It appears that any indication of liveliness, coquetry or sexual passion posed a threat to the calm waters...of familial equilibrium. This is shown by the complaint of Strepsiadis, **Aristophanes'** hero in the comedy "Clouds".

"My life on the farm was sweet as sweet could be...with the bees and the lambs.. and later I, a village boy, took someone from the town, full of fancy ideas of luxury and extravagance. When I married her and lay down next to her I smelled of wine-must, figs and fleeces, and she of rose water and myrrh and insatiable, wanton, voluptuous kisses."

Of course, this does not mean in any way that during the fourth century there were no husband and wives who fell in love and truly loved each other. We simply make note of the fact that passionate love did not play the role of match-maker in ancient marriage. Socrates in Plato's Symposium refers to an Athenian citizen, called Nikiratos, and stresses how deeply he loves his wife who loves him just as much. In any case, the greatest example from the period of mutual love and the dedication shared by a man and a woman is the case of **Pericles** and **Aspasia**. This relationship of course was not the typical marriage but rather one of concubinage because Aspasia came from Miletos. She was not Athenian nor from any city where she would have acquired the right of intermarriage from Athens so Pericles was not able to conclude a legitimate marriage with her. But they lived as man and wife and were dedicated to each other in a way that was scandalous...for the period. Their contemporaries could not accept that the great Pericles had given such a place of honor to a hetaira from Miletos!

The Platonic point of view concerning the relationship between man and woman, was that it was not worth calling it "eros" in the sense that we referred to it in the chapter on erotic love. The act, however, of the union of the male and the female led to fertilization and then childbirth and that made this act divine because fertility and childbearing insured a kind of immortality by itself. **Aristotle**, who was a student of Plato much later on, placed great importance on marriage.

He considered the couple equally responsible for the keeping of conjugal faith, recognized the rights of the woman as consisting not only of being a sexual partner but also that of an affectionate and trusted friend.

A woman decorating with branches of myrtle the jug that contains the water for the bride's prenuptial bath. The wall is hung with a wreath. (Representation from the 5th century B.C. at Eretria, Archaeological Museum of Athens).

The marriage ceremony

*B*ut since we are talking about marriage let us pause here to take a brief look at the wedding ceremony of the time and see just what it really meant when a couple in antiquity tied the knot.

First of all the best period to perform the ceremony was the month of Gamilonas, the seventh month of the Attican and Delian calender which corresponds to our January. It is said this was because this was the period when the first marriages were performed. The ceremony lasted for three days. It began with the future bride saying goodbye to her childhood, and dedicating her playthings to Artemis. These would have been small musical instruments, her dolls, a top, a headband, a kind of hair-net that had held her hair in place and frequently a lock of her hair. This was followed by the bridal bath. For that purpose, a boy who was related to the bride, (and both of his parents had to be living), would bring a large amphora filled with water from the river. For the bath of the Athenian bride, the water came from the river Kalirrohöe, and for the Theban girl the Isminos. The Trojan bride bathed in the river Skamandros saying: *"Skamandros, receive my virginity"*. This bath must have been taken after the sun set for we can see from the pictures painted on pottery, that torches were held during the procedure. The outer door and the house of the bride were decorated with garlands of flowers and fruit while the

Aristotle

Aristotle was born in Stageira, Chalkidiki in 384 B.C. and died in Chalkis in 322 B.C. He lived for quite a while in Athens where he became a student of Plato. He was the greatest philosopher of all time and his work is the basis of most modern science. All of science can be found in Aristotelian thought. His apprenticeship with Plato and his succession to the philosophical school laid the foundations for this brilliant development. His work, the study of which is of special interest all its own, consists of many divisions: Theology, Cosmology, Psychology, Biology, Ethics and Political Thought. The school he founded was called the Peripatetic school. Aristotle was also the teacher of Alexander the Great.

37

bride was lavishly dressed; she wore special shoes, a crown of myrtle or a diadem on her head and she was wrapped in a veil which covered her face.

Then there were sacrifices made to the hymeneal gods of marriage, Zeus, Hera, Aphrodite, Peitho and Artemis, and after that the wedding party sat down to the wedding meal.

The "νυμφεύτρια" (literally, "brides maid"), the woman who had undertaken the supervision of the marriage, led the bride with her face covered by the veil to the table. When the meal was finished there followed the "ανακα-λυπτήρια" (the "revealing") that is, the face of the bride was revealed, the act that signaled the official completion of the marriage ceremony. Then the groom offered her the "anakalyptιria" gifts. Afterwards, the bride's entourage, led by the aforementioned brides maid, and carrying torches, would take the bride to her husband's house where she would henceforth live. There the couple would be offered apples or quinces to eat and almost immediately led into the nuptial chamber. Standing outside the chorus of girls would sing the Hymnaion, the marriage song. The day after the wedding night, the bride would receive gifts from her parents and relatives.

Marriage in Sparta

Though in Athens marriage was not obligatory in the binding sense of the law, in Sparta and the Doric city-states, things were not like that at in the least. Above all else, the desire for good descendants was directly related to the freedom of the girls wearing the short tunics among the boys. As Plutarch mentions, Lycourgos, their law-giver, believed that the spectacle of semi-bare girls would lead young men into marriage or to put it another way as Plato would later say, *"the intense power of eros is stronger than even geometry"*.

In addition to all that, the laws provided a particularly embarrassing trial for the difficult and indecisive bachelor who kept putting off getting married. What was done to him?

Very simply, the laws required him to go out in the heart of winter without so much as a fig leaf on and walk around the main square singing a mocking song about himself in which he confessed that he found himself in this disadvantageous position because of his non-compliance with the law which prescribed marriage for all law-abiding citizens.

Aristophanes

Aristophanes was the most important poet of ancient comedy but also the most important in general in the fashioning of subsequent comedy. He was born around 450-444 B.C. and died in 385 B.C. Eleven of his comedies have survived which represent 1/4 of his total output. Among them the best known are "Clouds", "Birds, "Knights", "Archanians", "Lysistratus", "Frogs", "Plutus" and "Thesmomorphizousai". He is famous for the freedom of his language and for the jurisprudence he used in his realistic dialogues. He satirized nearly all the leading personalities of his age, even his teacher, Socrates.

But let us now turn to the Spartan marriage. As far as the wedding ceremony goes it was a complete washout. The bride was simply abducted and taken to the "brides maid" again who after closely cropping her hair, dressed her in a coarse, ugly dress, put men's shoes on her and then left her on a straw mattress alone in the dark, without even a chink of light.

The groom, after eating with his male companions as he did every evening, would slip out of the army camp and hurry off to meet his bride. The moment he entered the room he was expected to grab her, take her to the bed and consummate the marriage. When the couple felt sufficiently wedded he would run out again and return to his companions, making sure no one saw him along the way. And there he would sleep as on every other night. This was the way they would get together most of the time. It is said that there were couples in Sparta with children who had never really seen each other's faces.

We have examined, with as much understanding as possible, the "lukewarm" attitude of the majority of ancient men towards their better half....at least in regard to marriage during the classical period, and this attitude was perhaps in part justified by the successful relationships these men carried on with other women, a form of behavior acceptable during that period. Thus we cannot speak of male infidelity. Their "infidelity" was provided for by law. But what about the wife's infidelity? Here things were different. The adultery of the wife was labelled a crime and was grounds for divorce. Any man could get a divorce if he wanted to and could throw his wife out but this rarely happened. Why not? For the reason we mentioned previously: so the dowry would not have to be returned! To find oneself without a penny for no reason is no small matter! It has never been!

A bride receiving gifts from friends and relatives the day after her wedding.

39

In Sparta, however, (you are not going to believe this), where, generally speaking, they were rather backward in matters of culture, in certain other things they were very advanced indeed! If, of course, all this is true, as Plutarch says it is, then the Spartan women came out much better in the deal. They had relations with other men and indeed with the permission of their husbands! Look what Lycourgos, that demon legislator, dreamed up in the context of his endeavor to root out jealousy: if a young woman had an elderly husband he was permitted, if he so desired, to bring a young, robust man from a good family to his wife so that he might acquire, with this young man's assistance, a healthy son to raise as his own! A notable man was also allowed, if he met a beautiful woman, fertile, with many good qualities, but married, to borrow her from her husband so that she might also produce strong and healthy children for him! Here Plutarch has the law-giver saying to himself, when animals are bred, everyone carefully chooses the best males and even offers payment, then why should worthy women who happen to have an ill or witless husband not be able to avail themselves of the same privilege?

But since the relations of man and woman down through the centuries has never been that of a pure blood mare and her stallion for the reproduction of the race, the measure does not appear to have ever been tested, if of course we can even believe Plutarch that it was put into law.

If the image of marriage in antiquity that is emerging did not give much leeway to our protagonist, which in this book is Eros, remember that besides being a wife a woman had other roles that she played in the love life of the period, as we shall see below.

The wedding procession (painter of horsemen. Krater with its cone-shaped handles from 580-570 B. C.).

4

LOVE FOR SALE

Hetairas - Concubines
Prostitution

The hetairas

In our introduction to subjects such as the hetaira, the concubine and prostitution, there is perhaps no way to avoid the thought that in a society so prosperous and democratic as that of ancient Greece, the "oldest profession" would certainly not be missing. And indeed love for pay was very widespread. In the earlier societies prostitution did not begin as a commercial exchange but was part of a religious ceremony during which the girls sacrificed their virginity to the gods. The "ierodoules" (literally "sacred servants" but in actual fact another word for whore) got their name because they were holy courtesans in the service of the goddess of love, Aphrodite. Throughout their entire life these temple prostitutes exercised sacred prostitution like a religious duty which aimed at their becoming at one with the goddess. In antiquity hetairas are what unmarried women were called who lived freely with money they earned giving their body to men and offering them sexual favors (and bore similarities to both the courtesan and the geisha as was mentioned previously). This type of woman was very widespread. The Corinthian hetairas alone numbered over a thousand according to **Strabo**. During the Classical period, Corinth with its famous and expensive hetairas, was a pole of attraction that drew in a host of sailors, rich merchants, foreigners and Greeks who squandered their income there so that up to our days one still hears the phrase in Greece *"ου παντός πλειν εις Κόρινθον"*, that is, it is not easy for just anyone to go to Corinth. There was also religious prostitution in this town. Many Corinthian women were pious, they paid homage to the gods and gave them many gifts and dedications particularly those who made a lot of money. Most of the women who were employed in this profession were slaves who had been freed, or were penniless.

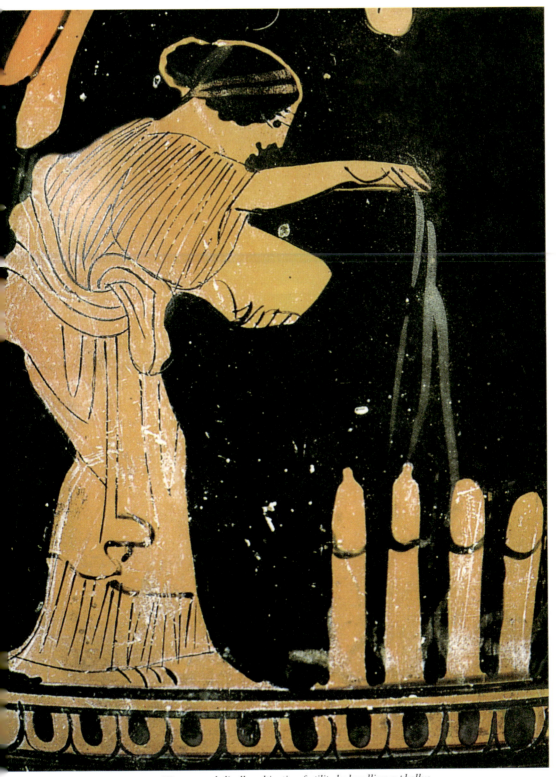

Woman symbolically cultivating fertility by handling a phallus.

Diphilos

An Athenian poet who also wrote satirical poems. He was one of the most famous poets of the new comedy. He lived in the 4th century B.C.

Alcibiadis

An Athenian politician and military leader who was born in 451 B.C. and died in 404 B.C. He was left an orphan at a very tender age and had Pericles as guardian, who was not able to supervise his upbringing as he should have with bad results for the moral personality of Alcibiadis, Athens and all Greece. Not even the philosopher Socrates was able to have a positive effect on him. He was an extremely handsome man of invincible charm and diplomacy and very brave and he would be distinguished for his valor in many battles, but in his personal life he was uncontrollable.
A transgressor of laws, he provoked public opinion with his displays and the scandals he created. He was an important orator, a genius of a general, but was utterly lacking in a moral basis.

Every hetaira exploited her natural beauty and charm, living in luxury because usually it was a rich man who was keeping her for an indefinite period of time. Thus, the hetaira could be regarded as a lover and not simply a whore, whom we will deal with below.

Even though we referred to the hetairas of Corinth as being expensive and renowned, the ones in Athens became famous because of their contact with noteworthy political men, artists, poets, and philosophers which resulted in the names of quite a few of them being connected to the names of important men.

Thus there are the well-known connections between **Praxiteles**, the famous sculptor, and **Phryne**, **Menandros**, the comic writer and Glykera, **Diphilos**, the poet with Gnathaina, and **Epicurus** with Leontion. **Alcibiadis**, who became famous for the passion which bound him to Timandra, who was the mother of the legendary **Laïs**, who was the lover of the Thessalian Ippolochos and rival of Phryne. The philosopher **Aristippos** the Cyrenian was connected with another hetaira also named Laïs who lived at the end of the fifth century B.C. which is why she is called the younger. The renowned orator **Hyperides** had also known Phryne at one time but later linked up with Myrinna who was considered to be one of the most expensive hetairas. It appears however that the oratory business was doing very well, and he probably did not have the time to write any speeches during that period as he was also keeping Aristagora and Phila.

He had set all three of them up in his houses in Athens, Piraeus and Corinth.

Besides their natural beauty these women paid close attention to their appearance and indeed in a way that made them stand out. **Lucian** describes it:

"...The hetairas and indeed even the ugliest of them, wore bright red clothes with the neck heavily ornamented with gold because they wanted to impress men with the luxury of their outfit and hide their imperfections with jewellery. They thought that their arms would become more beautiful if they covered them with the gleaming brilliance of gold and their ugly legs would become beautiful adorned with gold shoes and that their faces would become charming with gleaming jewellery."

Above we referred to couples of this kind whose names have gone down in history. Perhaps we should make special mention of the best known couple, Pericles and Aspasia, and rightfully so because Aspasia, this hetaira from Miletos, was the one who gave glory to the women of this class with her rare virtues. She had intellect, a good education and spiritual cultivation which impressed the men of her time. Pericles, to whom she was faithfully devoted, lived with her until his death and had a child by her. Many hetairas were educated and cultivated but this was by no means the general rule. Most of them supported themselves on their beauty and their femininity.

But this kind of erotic love, and at that time it was flourishing everywhere, independent of the intellectual accomplishments of the hetaira, was the spur to many relationships of mutual love and sincerity. After his wife Pythia died, the great philosopher Aristotle formed a relationship with Erpyllida and even had a son by her who was called Nikomachos, his father's name. The great warrior from the Battle of Salamis, Themistoclis, was the son of an Athenian citizen and a hetaira from Thrace, Avrotonon. But this did not prevent him from becoming a celebrated man in his time. Another general, Timotheos, was the son of the celebrated general **Konon** and a hetaira, which was made use of by his contemporaries to mock him. But Timotheos said: *"I am obliged to my mother who made me the son of Konon".*

Scene from an ancient symposium. Right, two young men, one of whom is playing "katava" (twirling a kylix without spilling any wine). Left, two adult men are getting drunk. Center, a naked hetaira is playing the double-pipe.

Hyperides

An Athenian orator from a rich family who lived from 390 B.C. to 322 B.C. Originally he was a compiler of court speeches in private matters where he acted as representative, but later he became involved in the public life of Athens. As a politician he was consistent and incorruptible with an exemplary manner and was a great supporter of Demosthenes. Quite a number of his works have survived which are characterized by simplicity and clarity. He used many words and phrases from comedy in his speeches and avoided rhetorical gimmicks because he was not trying to impress the public. His personality enjoyed the great esteem of his contemporaries.

Lucian

The most important writer of the 2nd century A.D. He was born in Samosata, Kommaginis, a district in Syria. He learned the Greek language and rhetoric and later studied Sophistic Rhetoric in Ionia. He visited many Greek towns and took part in the Olympic Games of Oratory where he was admired for his ability. He left behind important writings consisting of studies, speeches, dialogues and epistles.

Konon

An Athenian general who was active at the end of the 5th and the beginning of the 4th century B.C. He was a remarkable man and managed to resurrect Athenian power. During the Peloponnesian Wars he was made an admiral and carried out many important missions. His contemporaries considered him to be a courageous, moral and virtuous man.

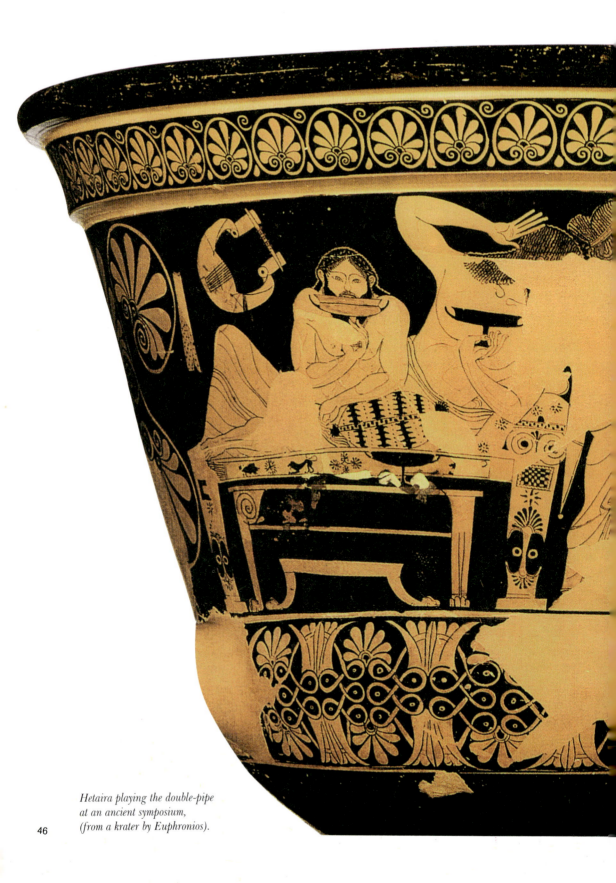

Hetaira playing the double-pipe at an ancient symposium, (from a krater by Euphronios).

Thus it it obvious that marriage was facing a crisis. How could it not be since couples rarely knew each other before the wedding and everything was handled by the parents while at the same time there were so many other women around, who were vivacious, intelligent, and attractive and whom the young men could find with such singular ease?

Of course the parents exhorted their children to marry in order to create a family or to concern themselves with their own intellectual cultivation, as can be seen in one of the "Hetairian Dialogues" by Lucian. The young hetaira Drosida had lost her beloved Kleinias who sent her a letter by a trusted friend which said among other things:

"That I love you Drosida I have the gods as my witnesses, but now I am avoiding you not from hate but from need, because my father has placed me with Aristainetos and he is teaching me philosophy and when he learned of our relations he reproached me severely and said it was unfitting that the son of Architelis and Erasicleia should be living with a hetaira and that it would be much better to choose virtue over sensual pleasure."

But let us return to our subject. Another category of hetairas were made up of the flute-girls, the dancers and the female harp-players who were called to symposiums to amuse the guests. There they would play guitar and flute, sing or dance and offer their company to the men who were having a good time. These "showgirls" were more or less the property of a master, who undertook their education and rented them out to private parties who were organizing an evening's entertainment. Of course at these symposiums the entertainment and the outrageous behavior often went beyond acceptable bounds, especially if the head of the house was also a reveller and obliged the guests to drink to excess. This frequently resulted in orgies with the hetairas, like those we see painted on the ancient pieces of pottery that have survived.

Laïs

There were two hetairas with the name Laïs. The oldest one came from Ykarra in Sicily and was the daughter of Timandra who was the partner of Alcibiadis. Contemporary with her rival Phryne in beauty, she ended up being stoned by the women of Thessaly where she had gone following her beloved Ippolochos. The younger one, a Corinthian (5th - 4th century B.C.) was greedy and acquisitive and was loved by Aristippos the philosopher. It is said that she only acted unselfishly with the philosopher Diogenes.

*I am an apple. And he's throwing me to you, Xanthippe,
the one who loves you.
Accept me, because it is fate that you and I shall wither.*

Plato

Hetaira lying on a couch from a vase by Euphronios.

Making the acquaintance and maintaining contact with these women was a very easy matter, since they were everywhere: in the agora, at the theaters, at the baths, in the temple of Aphrodite and walking through the streets, something that was strictly forbidden to virtuous women. As has already been mentioned, they wore characteristic attire that was deliberately provocative and had other distinctive attributes. Frequently these women also wore shoes with hobnails on the soles which left a design on the ground saying something erotic and suggestive such as "follow me", or "I'm waiting for you" to name but a few. I mention this so that certain interested parties will not think that the profession has made any important progress in the past two and one half thousand years! As for initiating contact an interested young man could try the "milovolia" approach in which he would show his interest in a particular hetaira by tossing an apple to her. (The "apple of his eye" perhaps!)

The clientele of the hetairas consisted of the richest young men of the period because the hetairas, as we have said, were expensive and their company cost an amount of money which the majority of men could not afford. For their part the hetairas had in this manner found a way of earning their livelihood and there were more than a few instances where the "profession" was handed down from mother to daughter as in the case of Timandra and her daughter Laïs. Poverty obliged quite a number of mothers to direct their daughters into this life in order to provide both for them and themselves.

This is the theme of another "Hetairian Dialogue" by Lucian. But let us see what Krovyli has to say to her daughter Korinna:

"— You see, Korinna, it's not as bad as you think, for a girl to become a woman. Now you know since you went to bed with that handsome young man and got one mna [100 drachmas], your first profit, and with that I am going to buy you a beautiful piece of jewellery.

— Yes, Mama! I want you to get me a necklace with red beads like fire, like Philaunidia has.

— Yes, I'll get you one like that. But hear some advice about what you have to do and how you should act with men because my daughter we don't all have the means to get by. It's been two years since your dear father died.....I had hoped that when you grew up...you'd have wealth, jewellery and servants.

— And how will I got that Mama? What are you trying to say?

— You can get it if you keep company with young men, make merry with them and sleep with them.

Like Lyra, Daphne's daughter?

— Yes!

— But...she's a hetaira!

— So what? Is that so bad? You'll get rich like she is and have lovers. Why are you crying, my child? Haven't you seen how many like her there are, how men love them and what kind of money they earn?"

But let us leave Krovyli to her catechism and emphasize once again the close bonds that some of the hetairas had with eminent Athenian men. Besides Aspasia who proved a wise counciler to Pericles and a comrade in all his work, we find Timandra, the hetaira of Alcibiades, who was so dedicated to him that when he died she arranged a magnificent funeral for him. The renowned Laïs left her profitable profession to dedicate herself body and soul to Ippolochos, the man she loved more than any other. The attitude of the orator Hyperides is also impressive for while enchanted by the charms of Phryne he was called upon to defend her in court with all his oratorical eloquence when she was charged with impiety. He saved her from certain death, because that was the penalty for that crime, by employing what became a famous ruse in antiquity, namely undressing her before the judges who were left dumbfounded by her divine beauty!

Phryne

She was a famous courtesan of the 4th century B.C. who was born in Thespies around 371 B.C. or 365 B.C. and died in Athens where she lived, in 310 B.C. Her real name was Mnisareti which means "she who remembers virtue"(!) and she was called Phryne after the "fryno", the toad, because she had a sallow complexion. Her exceptional beauty assisted her in her relations with many famous men, but her best known relationship, and the longest lasting, was with the sculptor Praxiteles.

The Venus de Milo.

Praxiteles

He was born in Athens at the beginning of the 4th century B.C. and lived until approximately 330 B.C. He was one of the most important sculptors of the period, the son of another sculptor, Kifissidotos. Most of what is known about Praxiteles has been compiled from the texts of ancient writers who referred to his work. Of his famous sculptures only a few originals have survived such as "Hermes with Dionysos" as a child, but there are quite a number of copies. His relationship with the courtesan Phryne characterized his life and his art as she was the model for many of his works. He also travelled to Asia Minor where he worked on the decorative reliefs on the columns of the temple of Ephesus which was considered one of the Seven Wonders of the Ancient World and which was burned down by Hierostratos in 356 B.C. His delicate artistic style was the inspiration of an entire school of artists.

Phryne, who was the model for her beloved Praxiteles' statues of Aphrodite, wrote him in a letter:

"...Of your many favors there is still one you haven't granted me: to come to me and lie down next to me here in the sanctuary where you erected my statue, together with Aphrodite and Eros. How is it possible to shame the gods that we ourselves have made?"

But what Phryne managed to accomplish with her beauty does not end here. She had accumulated so much wealth that when in 335 B.C. Alexander the Great demolished Thebes, she offered to rebuild it if the Thebans agreed to write over the entrance to the town: "Alexander pulled me down, Phryne the hetaira re-erected me". But this ambition was never realized because the Thebans were afraid that her glory might influence their wives to follow her example, as Kallistratos informs us. Nevertheless, her divine beauty inspired Apellis' picture "Aphrodite Emerging" when during the festival held in honor of Poseidon at Eleusis she plunged naked into the sea with her hair streaming behind her.

It appears that no man was indifferent to a beautiful hetaira and quite a few who only knew of one by rumor wanted to get to know her in person. Socrates set off to make such an acquaintance, according to **Xenophon**, but when he went to visit the breath takingly beautiful and rich hetaira Theodoti he soon found himself giving her advice on the pursuit of clients, since a host of lovers, as he himself supposedly said, when he saw the luxury she lived in, certainly represented greater profit that one could get from many herds of sheep! Of course Theodoti did not let the opportunity to seek the help of Socrates in this matter go by. It does not require a great deal of intelligence for one to realize that a place that Socrates frequented would attract a multitude of men!

Except, he said, he was already occupied himself with lovers of his own and he ended up by avoiding the proposal. *"I'll come when you call me, unless there happens to be someone with me that I love more than you".*

The Aphrodite of Rhodes.

Aphrodite meeting Eros (Cupid). Hellenistic figurine (Berlin).

Demosthenes

The Concubines

The concubines were another class of women who associated with men during that period. They cohabited in the same house with a man but without being married to him. **Demosthenes** put things in perspective, to a degree at least, by defining the meanings in his speech called "Against Neiara"

"We have hetairas for sensual pleasure, concubines for our daily bodily needs and legal spouses to give birth to pure children and to be faithful guardians of the home."

So we can draw the conclusion that the concubine was something between a hetaira and a wife, that she was established in the man's house, and that she could follow him in sacrifices or accompany him and serve him when he received his friends, things forbidden to a hetaira.

During the Homeric period, Trojans and Achaeans kept concubines, and considered as legitimate the children they bore them, but despite that gave first place to their lawfully wedded wives. In comparison, the Trojans, Priam being the most famous example, were polygamous while the Achaeans had only one legal wife. In the 5th century B.C. the men could, if they wished, keep concubines, but most of them remained monogamous.

Men and hetairas. Red-figured Attican vase painting from the 5th century B.C.

*Girl at washing vessel
(by Onisimos, 480 B.C.).*

53

Hetaira in an orgy with two men.

Your oaths are worth nothing.
I know them all, prodigal one.
Your plaits are witnesses,
drenched in scent.
I can see it your oh
so beady eyes
the ruined wreath
above your brow,
your hair tousled from orgies
and drunkenness.
Get out, lewd woman,
who prefers shame.
For you the harp
and the loud noise of rattles.

Meleager

Nevertheless, the rights of the concubine approached those of the wife, while any property she might have went into the common treasury of the man she was living with, without this being any kind of dowry. Concerning the position of the children of the concubines, during the Classical period they were legitimate only if the women were Athenian. Many poverty-stricken girls of that period took refuge in concubinage. During periods of war in particular a man's home commonly contained a concubine, in addition to his wife, because it provided an easy way to have children. From the 5th to the 4th century it was a very common practice to maintain girls for just this purpose, especially foreign ones.

Prostitution

*T*he oldest profession was also divided into classes since society has always been based on class. So the best off Athenians had their hetairas and their concubines, but what about the rest of the men, who were not so prosperous? For those there were the prostitutes. Prostitution shared the same roots with the hetaira, and meant the same thing: the women that exercised that profession sold their bodies and their sexual favours. What makes it different is that while the concubine belonged to someone, the hetaira belonged to a number of men, one succeeding the other after spending a certain period of time with her, be it long or short; the prostitute, conversely, set herself up in a dwelling and received clients continuously, one after the other, or went out looking for them as she still does today.

Decoration on a brass mirror with a scene from a whorehouse.

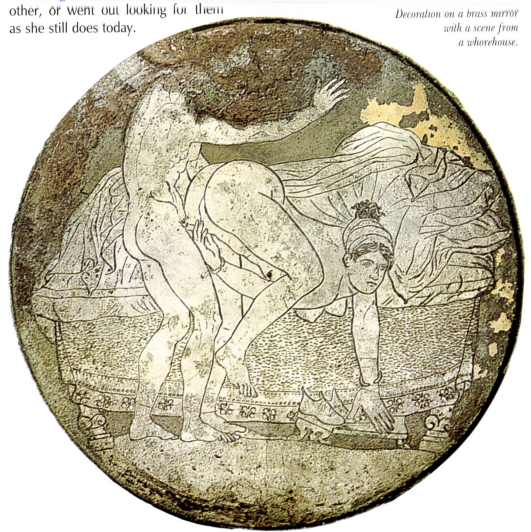

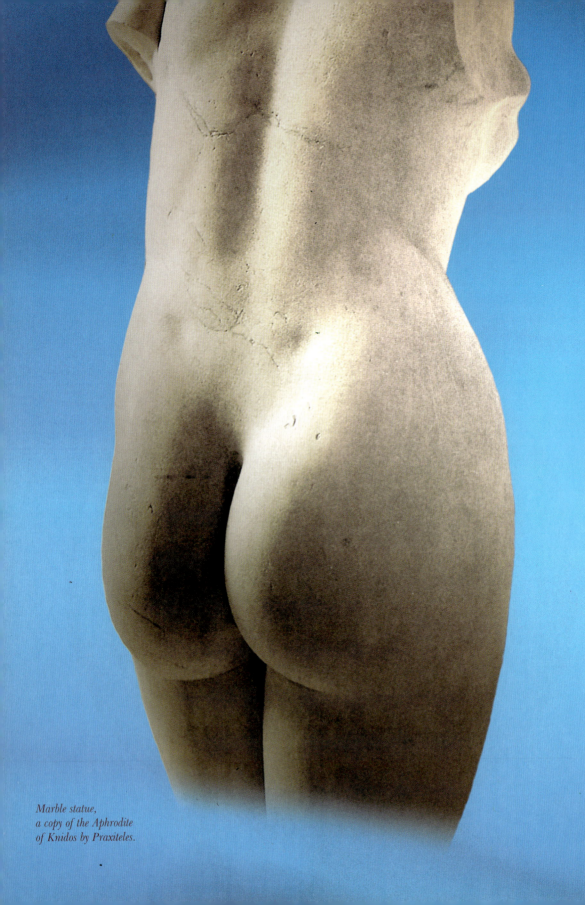

Marble statue,
a copy of the Aphrodite
of Knidos by Praxiteles.

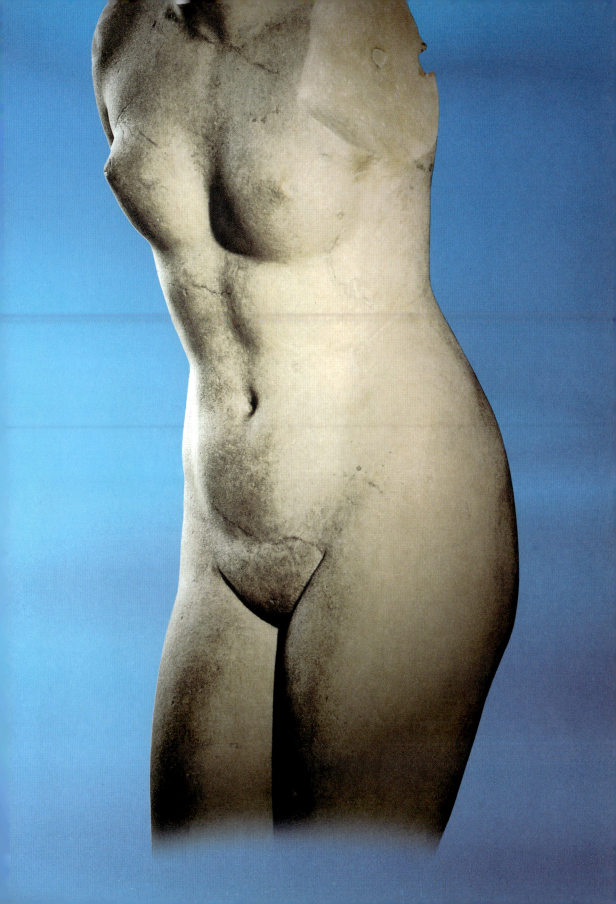

Archilochos

The word "porni" ("whore") first appeared in a fragment by the poet **Archilochos** in the 7th century B.C. and is derived from the ancient verb "pernimi" which means "to sell".

In Athens Solon was the first to establish houses of prostitution, at the beginning of the 6th century. The law-giver considered this measure necessary because the founding of such houses kept honorable women safe from the assaults of the unmarried men. These institutions were called, "whorehouses", "houses", "workshops", "homes of young maidens" and "places for display". The prostitutes were usually foreign women, primarily slaves, who would dress in transparent clothing or sit half-naked waiting for their customer. Each visit cost one obol (a coin of little worth). The women who worked in a private house of pleasure were of a higher social class than those in the public whorehouses. Nevertheless, this exchange was a source of profit for the Athenian government because the women who exercised this profession were obliged to pay a kind of tax, the "prostitution fee". Obviously, it has always been hard for anyone to escape the tax department. Thus, anyone who wanted to evade taxes had only one method: to have someone set her up in his house as a concubine.

Carnal scene depicted on pelike from the 5th century B.C. A man obviously aroused is making advances on a woman. Next to them is a rooster, symbol of the carnal.

Carnal scene
on the interior of a kylix.

These are some of the things that occurred in that society which enjoyed democracy and nearly all forms of liberty. All the stories about famous hetairas, or less exalted ones, about the squandering of fortunes, and about powerful and exclusive love affairs that led to the birth of children and went against the established practice of their period, lead up to one overwhelming conclusion: that the Greek man was moved by the female presence like nothing else. And even though the social and legal context restricted him, kept the woman from being a companion to him and disoriented him and confused him with all the moral imperatives or even the freedoms of his time, he, like the needle on a compass, always turned toward some female presence, through which to channel his sensitivity, and to give the proper dimension to the words of the great Demosthenes: "Woman is the most beautiful of creatures."

I swear, on the beauty
of Timos' curls
and the body of Dimo
that gives off a scent
that arouses me,
and I swear on the
affectations of Iliada
and even on this lantern,
witness to so much passion
that until the last breath
does pass my lips
yes, Love, I swear that
I will give it to you.

Meleager

5

SPECIAL FRIENDSHIPS BETWEEN MEN

The Spotlight...On the Male
Pederasty, viewed as a pedagogical institution
The position of the state - Relationships... for men only
The aim being Virtue

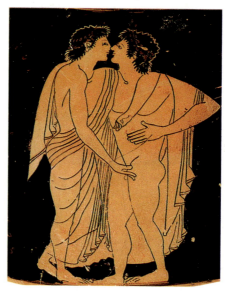

A beautiful world of measure and harmony is what Greek antiquity was and that becomes obvious if we take into account that its models remained the classical measures of comparison for everything that came after it down through the centuries. Thus, the Greeks always reacted with sensitivity to the aesthetically beautiful and that was true above all else for human nature. The healthy and harmonious body, whether it belonged to a man or a woman, was an object of admiration. But the restricting of women to the women's quarters and their relegation to a status of second-class citizen, contributed to the shift of the man's admiration to his beautiful male friends. In a very unambiguous manner, antiquity placed the man at the center of all intellectual life and interest, and focused on him alone! All this was connected to the previously mentioned "kalos kagathos" ("beautiful in body and soul, nobleness of character") and in the process became an ideal. Once having arrived at this formulation, there is no reason to let our imagination run riot with homosexual lovers and orgies and the like, because then we will be repeating the mistakes others have fallen into, mainly foreign researchers who in their translations of ancient texts have forgotten to pass their meanings through the filters which they would need apply to the thought and the perceptions of the period to which they belong. Is the problem the fact that they are dealing with a very ancient world? Is the problem that they are not Greeks themselves or that present-day thought is so mistrustful of customs which bring men so close to their fellow men? The word pederasty, for example, which in all languages means an erotic perversion, in classical antiquity was also used in the sense of a pedagogical institution, based on the pure and disinterested love of boys and not on homosexual relations with them. He who is unable to thoroughly examine the love of an ancient Greek for a naturally endowed boy, as something higher and sacred, loses the spiritual dimension of an entire world and remains estranged from all the miracles that this world represents to thought, philosophy and art.

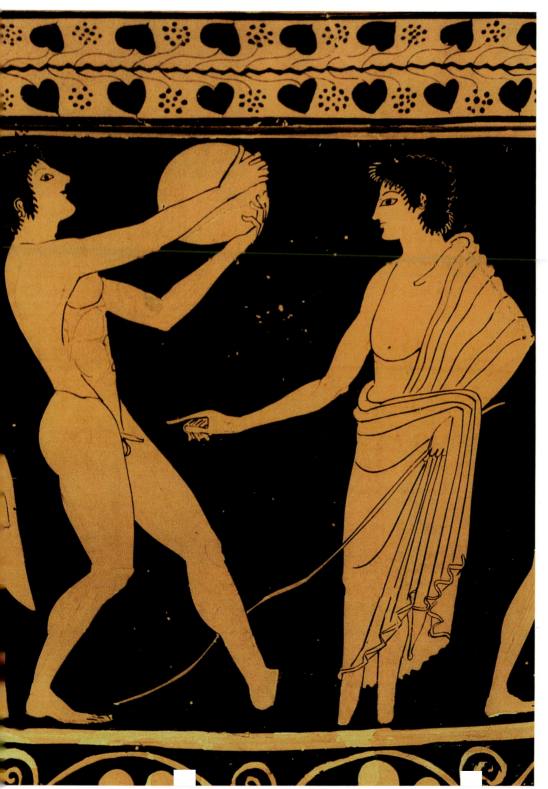

The athlete Antiphonis prepares to hurl the discus while his trainer gives him directions (from a vase by Euphronios, 4th century B.C.).

Since below we will continually be repeating the words "ερωτας" ("love, passion and the sexual act"), "εραστής", ("lover") and "ερωμένος" ("someone in love, lover"), we will be using quotation marks around these words when they have the meaning they had as analyzed in our chapter "A Word about Eros" and without quotation marks when we are referring to a carnal erotic relationship.

Pederasty viewed as a pedagogical institution

We previously said that the admiration of Greeks for beauty was so great that they deified it. They believed that in a beautiful body must dwell an equally beautiful soul, the cultivation of which it was necessary to attend to. And whatever else it may be, the work of Homer, the greatest poet of all time, is a hymn on beauty from one end to the other. Everywhere beautiful faces and young bodies are the protagonists and we are not speaking only of Helen who became the model.

Zeus, swept away by the beauty of the young Ganymede, has put down his sceptre and his thunderbolt, the symbols of his power. Ganymede is holding a rooster, a symbol of carnality (interior of a red-figured kylix from 460 B.C. (Ferrara, Museo Archeologico di Spina).

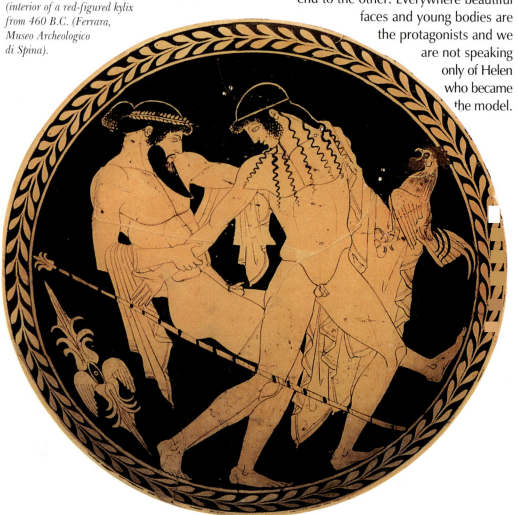

In Rhapsody 24 of "The Iliad" we see the king of Troy, Priam, the old father of Hector, coming to implore Achilles to give him back the body of his beloved son. Despite the misfortune and the devastation that is overwhelming him, his inner world still has room for the light awoken in him by his admiration for Achilles, that beautiful young man who has just killed his son! Such beauty had even over-whelmed Zeus himself, for he brought young Ganymede to be at his side, provoking various comments from antiquity till today concerning the nature of this "love". But Xenophon declares in his own "Symposium":

> *"My opinion is that Zeus brought Ganymede*
> *to Olympus not for his physical but*
> *for his spiritual beauty."*

Whatever the case may be, this action by Zeus strengthened even more what was considered axiomatic in the ancient world: that the beautiful was worthy of every form of respect and honor be it from the gods or men! And because beauty is first and foremost a characteristic of youth let us examine the so-called "pederasty" which from the 6th to the 4th century was the primary method of raising male youth. The suitable age for adolescents to receive this education was thought to be from twelve to eighteen. At that age they could be assigned to a man as their companion, who in agreement with the customs had to be over twenty years of age. So it was very good fortune and an honor for a boy when a citizen who enjoyed general public esteem, took him under his wing. Conversely, it was shameful for a boy if he did not have the honor of such a friendship.

Boy being taught to read by his teacher, from the drawings on a vase

Xenophon

A great Athenian historian and adherent of Socrates with a rich historical, philosophical and cultural series of works. Born around 431 or 430 B.C. in Attica he died around 351 B.C. He was the first "chronicler" of his time and wrote with ease of his personal views on everyone and everything. His writing was lucid and without bombast and was both expressive and simple. Among his experiences was his participation in the military campaigns of the Persian Ruler Cyrus the Younger against his brother Artaxerses along with Greek mercenaries. He narrated all that in his works. Besides his best known works, "Anabasis", and "Hellenica" among many others, he delivered testimony for the defense and justification of his teacher Socrates with the works "Apologia", "Symposia and "Memoirs".

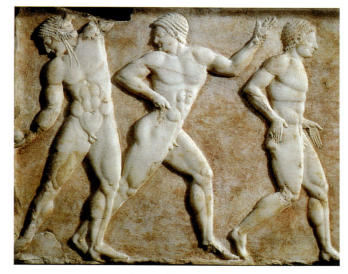

Relief of athlets at workouts.

*Representations
from the interior of a kylix.
Above: Young man at an ancient
symposium playing "katava".
Below: Another young man carries
amphoras full of wine.*

This relationship was also marked by the acquiescence of the father who felt proud when a worthy man chose his son. This man had the obligations of a guardian and mentor and exhorted the boy to all the manly virtues.

The custom had its roots in Doric practices. When the Dorians swept into Greece with their cruelty and their excessive male chauvinism, along with their contempt for women, which befitted a war-like people, they introduced the custom of "pederasty" because the men lived in army camps and by the very nature of things the older men became the teachers and the guides of future warriors.

The places where the beautiful young boys were especially distinguished were the arenas and training camps. Admiration for their beauty was the main stimulus for a man to proceed with the selection of a young man whose inner world he wished to mould so as to make him into the proper man.

Socrates, informed by an inner sense of purity, presented himself as a "lover" to his students because only someone who feels love for another is able to instruct him. Furthermore, the cultivation of the soul he needs so he will progress and prosper must have beauty as its aim. And as we said, the Greek "creed" that stated external beauty had to enclose a beautiful inner world was the stimulus behind every wise teacher. Nevertheless, in the so-called "pederasty" of the time there was love on a psychic level, a union of souls, not bodies. In its original meaning it was "eros" without the accompaniment of Aphrodite, as they said. The participation of Aphrodite is what characterized bodily love. It is a fact that pederasty, in the present sense, was then a punishable offense and the courts rigorously prosecuted it. Xenophon mentions in "The Lacaedamian Republic" that Lycourgos praised as the most worthwhile form of education, the admiration of a virtuous man for the soul of a child and his endeavor to shape him into a good fellow warrior, so that he could live well in his companionship. Conversely, he considered any kind of carnal passion for the body of a child to be a great source of shame. That is why the Spartans, showed temperance in their sensual pleasures and avoided that kind.

In Athens, the institution of "pederasty" was observed in the upper classes as well. The "lover", (the "erastis") who was an adult man, gave advice and all the knowledge he possessed from his own education and experience, to an adolescent "lover" and the adult was reimbursed, in his turn, by the enjoyment of the adolescent's beauty and his grace. And to be even more clear about this, sensual pleasure for a "lover" meant nothing more than watching the naked boy in the gymnasium!

The "lover" would offer him various gifts because of this friendship. These were usually game taken in hunting, a rooster, a hare, or a dog, or perhaps a vase dedicated to the young man on which the older man had written comments in his praise.

To a callous man give
not your kiss
nor your companionship.

Archilochos

The virtuous will teach
you virtue.
If you mix with the bad ones
you will lose even your mind.

Theognis

Adult man with a beard presenting
a hare to his young friend
as a gift.

Decorations from the interior of a kylix.
Above: Naked young man preparing
to fill the wine cup from the krater.
Below: Young man filling the wine
cup from the goat-skin.

The discussions they had dealt with a great range of subjects whose aim was to inspire the youth with moral values, obedience to the laws, the ways of proper behavior, nobility and ethos so that he would become a courageous and moral man. At the same time he accompanied him to the theater, cultivated his taste for art and helped him in the development of his judgement.

The adolescent was obliged to respect his mentor, and deeply esteem him and to show by his behavior how obliged he was to him.

But we must not neglect mentioning that the first and primary part of the spiritual bond between the lovers was complemented by a second part, which consisted of discreet erotic expressions of bodily contact on the part of the "lover". This is what we have garnered, mainly from various depictions found on pottery in which one can observe a man caressing the genitals of a youth. Lover and beloved are always in a position facing each other. It is obvious there were "unwritten" laws which regulated the behavior of the "lover". The youth first of all was to avoid even the slightest contact with the "lover" until he proved that he was worthy of such a concession while he himself never sought any pleasure from such a caress. He maintained a

Scene depicting
a man erotically caressing a boy.

Man and adolescent in a scene from the 6th century B.C.

serious and modest demeanor, even while being touched and did not so much as raise his eyes to look at his companion. An attitude of enjoyment on the part of a boy was considered reprehensible.

In the most extreme cases where the adult ejaculated this was done against the young man's thighs and always in the position we just mentioned. It was strictly forbidden to assume any posture that facilitated contact with the backside of the loved one or introduction of the male member into any part of his body. The adolescent, as we said, did not participate in the carnal embrace; he was only allowed to accept tender caresses from his older companion but no contact that would debase him into playing the role of a woman, or a carnal object. He was tomorrow's citizen and must not be dishonored. The dominant role when it came to making "advances" belonged solely to the man and since the adolescent was destined to become such a man, it would be debasing to find himself in the passive position of humiliation and subjection. Just how disgraceful they considered this to be is shown by a representation on an Attican red-figured vase. This depicts a Persian in a posture which is declared by the inscription underneath. "I am Evrymendontas. I have submitted myself." Behind him there can be seen arriving a Greek gesturing with his genitals in such a way there can be no doubt as to his intentions. This pot, painted after the victory of the Athenians at the river Evrymendontas around 460 B.C. triumphantly proclaims, just as their contemporaries do today, when their team wins at soccer: *"We screwed the Persians!"*

Thus only one who is defeated and humiliated would suffer such an act! Those who had a tendency toward this form of behavior were cursed roundly. The kinaidos (= kino tin aido = "shake the pudenda", i.e. passive homosexual), the katapuygonas (= "lewd fellow" the unnaturally licentious), the kataproktos, evryproktos or lakkoproktos (= words for the anus indicating a lewd passive homosexual) were all epithets for these people who lived on the margins and were socially unacceptable.

Marble stele from Sifnos with the head of Hermes (a phallic similarity) (520 B.C., Athens, Archaeological Museum).

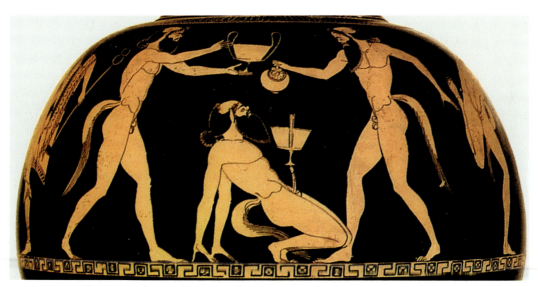

Orgy with Satyrs.

Some students or even ordinary readers have concluded from inscriptions that have survived that the relationships between "lovers" and "loved ones" were purely homosexual. We will not go so far as to say that there were not, in every period, deviations from the rules, but in terms of the inscriptions, care is perhaps needed. In those days it was very common for someone to write about his male friend *"O Lysias is beautiful, yes!"* or *"Theognis is beautiful, in the name of Zeus!"*. At the same time inscriptions have also been found that have a highly derogatory tone to them and which can lead to certain conclusions. For example, *"Kimon here had intercourse with Amotimonas"*. If we bear in mind that not even during that period did they talk very easily about certain subjects, except when trying to humiliate someone, we are led to other considerations. In the chapter on "Love for Sale", in one of Lucian's "Hetairian Dialogues" we meet the young hetaira Drosida who had lost her lover, the young Kleinias, because his father had handed him over to the philosopher Aristanetos for instruction. We will remember from the letter Kleinias wrote that the teacher had forbidden his pupil to have relations with a hetaira.

So what do you think Drosida did then? She went on the counterattack the following day, with the assistance of her girl friend who could write, and on a wall at Kerameikos where the young man's father was accustomed to passing by, said that *"Aristainetos is corrupting Kleinias"*. So much for inscriptions and what they reveal and...don't reveal.

I am not a pederast.
What pleasure do you see
in the love of adolescents?
To be always the one to give
and never to receive!
But "the one hand washes
the other" and that's why
for my bed
I chose a woman.
What do I want with hairy,
male legs.

Meleager

The position of the state

*T*he fact that "erotas" is presented as something worthy of praise in terms of public opinion, in a sense that would not lower one's social reputation, did not mean that parents and law-givers did not worry about the minority who might exploit young men for the purpose of corrupting them. Parents always took measures to assure that their children were not shamed and the state also took care to guard the high moral standards of education.

The laws of Solon obliged the parents not to send their boys to school before the sun rose and to take them home from their lessons before it set so they would not face the danger of being alone on the streets. Entrance to the school was forbidden to other young men and to strangers. But from Aristophanes we also learn about the modest customs of the generation of warriors who fought at the Battle of Marathon.

"They sat very respectfully in the arena of the training center, careful to maintain a decorous posture, and when they got up they also took care to smooth out the sand so they would not leave the marks of their private parts and thereby cause someone to feel disgust nor did they smear themselves with oil from the navel down leaving a simple tuft to bloom, like the fuzzy bloom on a quince."

Linos the musician teaching the lyre to Iphiclis, the brother of Heracles.

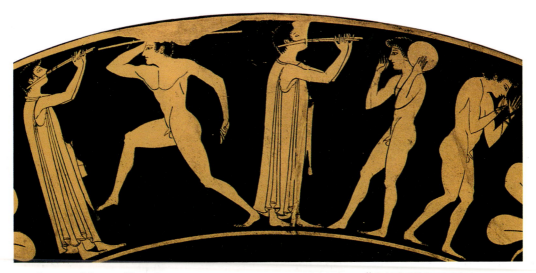

The republic itself took very stern measures to protect young boys from all kinds of machinations, and even from their own parents who had authority over them. If a father or guardian handed over his child to some pervert for carnal contact, taking money in exchange, the adolescent would not be prosecuted but rather the guardian.

The boy for his part, would be freed thenceforth of every obligation of housing and looking after his guardian in later life. The only obligation he would have toward him would be to arrange his funeral since that was an inalienable law for all the dead which showed a respect rooted in religion. Strict penalties in accordance with the laws of Solon and penal prosecution existed for anyone who incited young children, female and male, free or slave, into debauchery.

From all this we conclude that "pederasty", examined from a moral point of view, had its own special character which was maintained on an aesthetic, religious and educational basis. Its purpose was the maintenance of institutions, and the elevation of social and personal virtue with the assistance of the republic and was considered to be an important pedagogical factor. Without a doubt we are dealing with a society which placed moral values at a premium.

Aristotle, who dealt with the idea of physical pederasty very harshly and included it among the corrupting practices, said characteristically, *"lovers do not look at any part of the body except the eyes, where modesty dwells"*. (Fragment 91, "To the Athenians", XIII, 564 b).

Scene of athletes training in a gymnasium on an Attican red-figured kylix by Epiktitos (520 B.C., Berlin, Antiken Museum). One athlete is preparing to hurl the javelin and the other the discus. Athletes in tunics set the rhythm.

First of all, he should be a child and when the moment comes he will learn carnal pleasures from a woman and at the proper age will find the solution on his own.

Solon

Relationships for Men Only

*I*n various museums, as well as in many pictures in books, our eye is frequently caught by the salacious scenes painted on pottery depicting orgies between Satyrs or among Satyrs and Maenads and which provoke the usual commentary. It would be ingenuous to maintain in what would be a kind of oxymoron that *"we have discovered... innovations in antiquity"* since in our time international pornography has produced subject matter that boggles the mind. In any case all the erotic passions have been known fully from the very beginning, wherever there have been people. The fact that these pots have become the source of misinterpretation is something worthy of discussion because certain homosexual attitudes are considered to be "proof" of the Greek way of life. And first of all, it should be clarified that the representations of Satyrs, Sileni and Maenads belong to the sphere of mythology where the fanciful disposition of each artist had a wide field to work in. Furthermore, the entourage of Dionysos was supposed to be wild and uninhibited because these mythical beings symbolized the orgiastic spirits of nature. The god Priapos, with his enormous phallus, as well as the other phallic effigies, were directly connected to a male-dominated society, with its pursuit of power but also with fertility. Consequently, these depictions do not describe a reality but serve other artistic purposes.

Pictures which depict men at a banquet giving themselves over to carnal embraces, are always concerned with the activities of adults and there is nothing that shows that they have taken anything from a real event through the means of art. The imagination of artists has always been unfettered and it creates according to its inspiration, the personal idiosyncrasies of the artist or his satiric temperament. But even if there were a smidgen of truth in any of these drawings, they would be isolated instances certainly and would not characterize the whole nor even a certain period of time in antiquity. This is even more the case if we take into account that Greece, and indeed the large urban centers, such as Athens, were not inhabited only by Athenians, but also by a multitude of foreigners, and colonials, slaves and freed slaves.

Satyr on a krater by Euphronios.

*Part of a gigantic marble
phallus symbolizing
the generative force that Eros
brings to nature (Delos).*

Theokritos

The greatest and most charismatic poet of ancient Greek literature during the Alexandrian period. It is thought that he was born around 315 - 305 B.C. in Syracuse where he lived for some time but he lived in Kos as well. He was distinguished for his bucolic poetry and he wrote many "Idylls" as his histories were called. His heroes live in nature and his language is Ionic with Doric forms in the idylls while his poetry is basically Doric with Aeolian elements.

But let us now speak of these particular relations between Greek men that have caused so much discussion. The study of the Homeric epics, do not leave the slightest doubt that for Homer and his period homosexuality was virtually unknown. There is nowhere in these works the slightest hint of it either among the gods or the human beings. The poet who describes with such eloquence beauty, grace and the love of men and women, no matter how discreet he might have wanted to be, would have certainly mentioned such a relationship somewhere. Furthermore, eros with or without quotation marks was something that was talked about in these early societies.

Concerning the matter of Zeus and Ganymede the only thing mentioned is that the divine beauty of the young man was a factor in his being taken to dwell among the gods as Zeus' wine-bearer. The relationship of Achilles with Patroclos in Homer represents the ideal friendship between men, typified by a rare purity.

The endeavor made later on to examine this relationship through a different prism did not convince most people because in the figure of Achilles was embodied the masculine ideal of his period: he was the alluring man who seduced Deidimeia, he was the fiery lover of Brisida, the much beloved husband of Polyxeni and the chivalric admirer of the brave Panthesileias, all of them women. As for the relationship of Hercules with Ylas, **Theokritos** writes in his idylls:

"Hercules with his heart of iron, was mad about a young boy, the graceful Ylas, with his hair all in curls. He taught him, like a father his favorite son, everything that he himself had learned about being brave and worthy of the Muses. He never let him leave his side...he wanted to fashion him according to his own desires...so he would become the perfect man".

In the Theban cycle we observe that Hera sends to Thebes the monstrous Sphinx to punish Laïos for his guilty love of the beautiful Chrysippos, the son of Pelops. Laïos is presented as an example to be avoided in Plato's "Laws" where in his most mature work he condemns carnal love between men and notes the bad end that Laïos came to and the tribulations suffered by his family.

The aim being Virtue

All the actions of the ancients were characterized by their transparency, for instead of covering up human passions, they endeavored to explain them. That is what Plato was trying to do in his "Symposium", through the mouth of Aristophanes. And here is the myth:

Once, a very long time ago, humans were double beings. Monstrous creatures who were stuck together back to back. These pairs were also of different combinations: there were men with women, men with men and women with women. Zeus and the other gods, in order to deal with these creatures who, united as they were had immense power, divided them in two. Since then, each of the separate parts has been trying to find "its other half", as we still say today, without even knowing what we are talking about. So, if a man was once connected to a woman, he will look for her. If he was united to a man he would not feel complete if he did not find him. As for the woman who is attracted to other women, well, this only occurs because she was once joined to another woman!

But let us leave those people who had to "straighten things out" as best they could in the world given them and examine some other points in the Platonic Symposium.

"Those who have within them the breath of "eros" prefer that which is more robust and has spirit. The proper "eros" does not lead you to pederasty because boys are immature and do not have judgement."

"He is thought "unworthy" who is in love with someone because he is beautiful for this is the love of the body and not the soul and this kind of eros soon takes wing and leaves. But the one who is "in love" with good character will remain a "lover" throughout his entire life".

Athenian statue of Heracles, from the 4th century. B.C.

Aschines

Another Athenian orator and a political opponent of Demosthenes who lived from 389 - 314 B.C. He is listed among the ten orators of the Attican Canon. As he came from a poor family he does not appear to have studied in the schools of his time but he drew a great well of knowledge from his study of the tragedies when he was involved in the profession of actor. He was an athlete and a brave warrior. Originally he was an opponent of Philip, the Macedonian king, but later after the concluding of peace between Philip and Athens, he developed a more conciliatory disposition and lined up in favor of his policy. The style of his speeches was delicate, their expression lively and their content practical.

Ancient Athenian warrior with helmet and shield who is obviously holding a spear.

This ethic that was built up around "eros" in relationships between men, with virtue as their aim, was the source of great valor and the secret of male friendship. As difficult as it is to understand today, this love had nothing humiliating, corrupting or effeminate about it. It was the force that gave rise to heroism and it directed valor to remarkable heights. Because "eros" lends a divine spirit and makes men braver, and does not only not lead to anything unseemly but is also the best way to maintain the line of battle. And indeed, the salvation and victory of the warriors lay in their friendship which formed the line. A brilliant proof of this assertion concerning this particular form of male behavior is the battle of Chaironeia where the Sacred Company of Thebes fell fighting on the field of battle. They were sarcastically called the "company of lovers", by those who were envious of the rise of Thebes to power.

However, the victorious Macedonian King Philip could not hold back his tears when he saw three hundred lifeless bodies before him. They had fallen to the last man after fighting bravely, all wounded in the chest. Deeply moved, Philip said:

"A curse on those who have treacherously hinted that such men could have done or accepted anything vile".

The fifth century of the classical period may be touted for its democracy and the freedom enjoyed by its citizens but this does not mean there was moral lassitude, as some would have it. Furthermore, the law against homosexuality which had been preserved in the speech by **Aeschines** "Against Timarchos", leaves no room for misinterpretation.

"If an Athenian man is shown to be a passive homosexual, he should not be permitted to be elected one of the nine notables, he should not receive the office of priest nor should he become a trustee of the deme, nor assume any official capacity at all, neither internally nor externally nor in the clergy, nor elected, nor express an opinion nor enter the public shrines, nor wear a wreath on the customary holidays nor go to the sprinkling of the agora. Indeed if he does any of these things while it has been proven in the courts that he is homosexual, he ought to be punished by death".

Silver coin with Philip on it (4th century B.C.).

Relief base with depictions of athletes from the 4th century B.C. from the Acropolis.

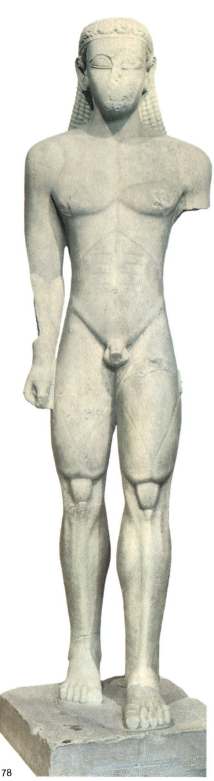

What Athenian man of the 5th century B.C. would have wanted the kind of life predicated by such a dishonorable position? Timarchos on whose account Aeschines referred to that law, was not only shown to be a passive homosexual but in addition a prostitute. That is, he also took money which made the Hellaia judges knit their brows in consternation: the man who does not hesitate to sell his body would think it no great matter to sell out the interests of his country!

But whatever the case, Timarchos could not stand the shame and committed suicide.

With laws as harsh as this, it would have been very difficult for the lax climate, that some have imagined, to have ever existed.

But since it is not our intention to show any form of bias, we accept the fact that homosexual relations between men, like all human failings, have existed in all places and at all times. Which leads us to the consideration that anything that occurs between two people that is completely consensual is a personal matter — and respected — and we do not exempt Greece from this rule.

Furthermore, why were such phenomena not satirized in the works of Aristophanes if he knew of them? But these incidents did not constitute the rule in any instance, nor could they have characterized ancient Greek society and even more to the point there is no way Greece could be viewed as having been the cradle...of perversion!

This title, to the degree it refers to the ancient world, belongs unquestionably to Sodom and its neighbors. The ancient Greeks were of the opinion that passive homosexuality came from the Phoenicians and that is precisely what they meant when they said of someone that "He was acting Phoenic" ("foinikizei").

In closing we believe that the moral evaluation of the male character in both public and private life is the basis from which everything that was created by ancient Greek civilization got its start, and which will be admired as long as there are people to admire it.

The famous ancient Kouros of Sounion.

An adolescent playing the double-pipe for entertainment of those at an ancient symposium.

6

EROTIC FRIENDSHIPS BETWEEN WOMEN

Lesbian love - The love of Sappho

Lesbian Love

*I*t is already obvious, from all that we have said, that even in very ancient times, there was nothing un-known about the human body, erotical-ly speaking. Unquestiona-bly, the same holds true for love bet-ween wo-

Women playing "astragalous", considered to be a woman's game.

men. The myth of Plato's Symposium with its peculiar "anthropology" refers to this kind of relationship in an effort to explain it. However, there is very little information about these particular relationships between women. The fact that woman were neglected by their husbands leads to the notion that the common alternative solution of another man would have been difficult as they faced the problem of restricted move-ment, so they would either have to contend with constant sexual frustration or find relief in old-fashioned masturbation.

This notion gains credence from the exis-tence of special "equipment" designed for this purpose. In short, in Miletos, which was the commercial center of wealth and luxury, certain specialized craftsmen made the "vauvones" or "olisvous" which were mod-els of the male organ, fashioned of soft leather.

The hetairas, and everyone else who knew of their existence, and had access to a supply of them, used these dildoes as instru-ments of self-gratification.

In regard to the erotic relationship between women which was called "lesbian love" ("λεσβιακός έρωτας") or "lesbian-ism" ("λεσβιασμός") it is known that it had its origins on the island of Lesbos where these friendships between women were at a more developed stage.

Woman uncovering a receptacle full of phallus-like objects while holding a winged phallus in the shape of a bird.

Sappho

Sappho of Lesbos was the greatest lyric poet of early Greek antiquity. She was born between 617 and 612 B.C. She is mentioned as having been born both in Mytilene and in Ephessos, both towns on the island of Lesbos. Sappho lived in Mytilene and married Kerkylas, a wealthy man from Andros. She had a daughter, Kleïda. Political disturbances drove her into exile in Sicily. She returned to Mytilene in 585 B.C., now a widow, and created a circle round herself of her female friends and students. Her poems are written in the Aeolian dialect. She also wrote songs. She was a contemporary of Pittacus the tyrant of Mytilene, one of the Seven Wise Men, and of Alcaeus, whom we have already met. Her work is very important and her verses mature and sensitive and of enduring value down through time.

Alcaeus

A lyrical and melodic poet from Mytilene. He is thought to have reached the height of his powers in 598 B.C., and he was a contemporary of Sappho and Solon. Together with his brother Antimenidas, he became involved with the resistance to the island's tyrant, Pittacus. From the few examples of his poetry extant it appears that he visited Delphi and Egypt. He wrote political poems, love poems and poems that were sung at symposiums. His poetry is quite remarkable and while it is terse in expression, it contains tenderness, power and majesty.

Lesbos is the homeland of the famous poet **Sappho** to whom are attributed these activities and their spread. Since Sappho lived in companionship with young girls for pedagogical purposes, many contemporaries, or those who came later, assumed that she was the one who established this perverted form of behavior among women. But this has no basis in truth, as we shall see below.

The Lesbians, as the homosexual women were called, in antiquity were called "τριβάδες" (from the verb "τρίβω" = "to rub") and took part in erotic embraces with members of their own sex.

There are no relevant depictions on pots, perhaps because the phenomenon was of such limited extent, but also perhaps because it was not of any particular interest to the artists of the period.

From Lucian's "Hetairian Dialogues" there is one very characteristic one, between two women friends, Klonarion and Leaina, which describes relations such as these with sufficient clarity.

"**Klonarion:** What's all this I hear about you, Leaiana? They say that Megilla, that rich woman from Lesbos has made love to you like a man and that you're sleeping together and who knows what all. Ah! I see you're blushing! So it's the truth then?

Leaina: It's true, Klonarion, I'm ashamed to say, but it's something really strange.

Klonarion: In the name of Demeter, what do you mean? What does she want from you? What are you doing? Aren't you going to tell me? Is this what friendship means?

Leaina: I consider you my friend, better than any other, but what can I say? That woman has very manly tastes.

Klonarion: I don't understand, are you a Trivas? They say there are a lot of these manly women on Lesbos that don't want to do it with men but go with women as if they were men.

Leaina: That's what she's like.

Klonarion: So explain it to me...

Leaina: They had a dinner party, she and Dimonassa the Corinthian. When it was late and they were drunk, Megilla said to me: it's time to go to bed. Stay here Leaina and sleep with us; we'll put you in the middle.

Klonarion: Did you stay? What happened?

Leaina: In the beginning they kissed me like men. Then Megilla...took off a wig I hadn't realized she was wearing and her hair was cropped close to her head, like a powerful athlete. I was scared. Have you ever seen such a gorgeous young man before, Leaina? she asked me. I don't see any young man here, Megilla, I answered. Don't call me by a feminine name — I am Megillos and I have married Dimonassa. I couldn't keep myself from laughing, Klonarion! But I said do you have that thing that men have and do to Dimonassa what you should? She said, I don't have it but I don't really need it. Then are you a hermaphrodite, I asked. No she said...come on and you'll see. I let her do it in the end since she begged me so much.

Klonarion: But what did she do? Tell me, I want to know!

Leaina: Don't ask any more. It's so disgusting that in the name of Aphrodite I'll not say another word".

*The Muses all in all are nine, some say
but it is wrong!
There is a tenth,
look here: it is Sappho
from Lesbos!*

Plato

Two naked hetairas. The seated one is stroking the pubic area of the other. Rare scene, from the 5th century B.C.

One time your mother, Kleïda, told me
for a girl your age
a piece of jewellery is lovely, suitable
red ribbons to tie hair.
But if she has pure blond hair
from the shining of torches
more luminous
she is dignified by wreathes woven of flowers..."

Sappho

The love of Sappho

We saw in the institution of "pederasty" that the initiation of the adolescent into virtue by his older friend contained everything that was necessary for the formation of the personality of a man. Women, however, were excluded from social life and nothing of theirs was considered worthwhile because no matter how cultivated they might be, they had no share in any part of public life and therefore had nothing to contribute to its notion of virtue. The question of what the measure for the evaluation of female virtue was and how this virtue could be proven within the company of the woman, was never to find an answer.

Sappho was the first to dare, by following the male models of "pederasty", to make "Sapphic love" a demonstration of virtue for the cultivation of the beautiful girls of Lesbos. Ancient writers mention that in Lesbos as elsewhere in Aeolia, there were the cultural preconditions for the woman to apply herself to other interests, outside the house. Something both of note and very innovative was the custom that was established on Lesbos of having beauty pageants. These contests were held every year at the temple of Hera along with a series of ceremonies and sacrifices. Here we have something similar to the Olympic Games: female athletes who competed in their sector for their own virtue.

The girls of that far-off period competed, for the honor of Hera, at beauty, grace, singing, dancing and even running. Thus, while in all the rest of Greece women lived a life limited to the women's quarters, on Lesbos there were the preconditions for the female cultivation of virtue. The circle of Sappho's students was not the only one; there were other women who gathered girls around themselves, but she was the most important of them. They later said about her that she was for young women what Socrates was for his male students.

Woman holding mirror, from the 4th century B.C., Archaeological Museum of Taranto Italy.

Alcaeus and Sappho on an Attican krater, circa 470 B.C. (Munich, State collection of Antiquities and Sculpture).

*"Mnisidiki is more
shapely than
delicate Gyrinna; ah,
my gracefull, never have
I met a woman who gave
herself more airs than you..."*

Sappho

*Marble stele with kore in relief,
probably from Paros.
She holds a box, the cover of which
has fallen to the floor.
Her peplo hangs loose at the side.*

Faced with a male-dominated society where military masculinity was the supreme virtue, Sappho dared to oppose this with the lyricism of her feminine sensitivity, as expressed through her tender verses:

*Some say the fairest thing on this black earth
is men marching others say horsemen
others say it would be ships
but I say she who one loves best.*

Sappho has been slandered for female homosexuality, for Lesbian love, as we described it above. These charges have never been proven and those who have maintained it have based their theory on verses which are themselves only fragments. But these fragments do not even prove it. If there was any "love" on her part for young girls it would correspond to the Platonic model, a love of what was still physically unfulfilled. The life that Sappho chose was not in any sense one on the margins. She was married, had a daughter, fell in love with men, and in the end died for the love of a man.

The girls who studied beside her learned dance, music, the secrets of feminine grace, manners, social behavior and what's more that is why their parents entrusted them to her, not so they could learn the secrets of love, as some have alleged. Even for Lesbos and Aeolia, where women displayed considerably more progressive behavior for those times, that would have been extreme, and none of the parents would have given their consent for their daughters to study with her.

These girls were after all getting prepared for their weddings. Indeed Sappho often took part in the formal ceremony of the marriage of her students. The nostalgia and grief which infuse her verses over the departure of her girls, is a natural emotion of an older woman, of a teacher who has watched a child change from a little girl to a woman who is now setting off on a new life with a husband or is going to another place to live. Is not the praising of beauty, love and virtue in absolute agreement with the meritocratic perceptions of the world of men? But is not "eros" as well, in the way we defined it our chapter "A Word on Eros", socially acceptable? But it was a provocation for her period, the 6th century B.C. to have a woman with such a brilliant personality!

Her contemporaries treated her with suspicion since she spoke openly of her emotions. The freedom her work is imbued with was something practically unknown in her period. There was no ground to develop such initiatives except malicious commentary.

The love of the proud Phaonas proved fatal for Sappho. Both Strabo and Menandros mention that on Lefkas, where the poetess had taken refuge, there was a temple to Apollo Lefkatas with an altar where the famous "Leap into the Sea" took place. That is where unrequited lovers made the supreme sacrifice to be delivered from the pain of love. And that is where Sappho took the leap, unable to face her dilemma. Her tender lines still bear a rare freshness so many centuries later:

"Sappho's leap into the sea"
(copperplate).

Like the sweet apple at the tip of the branch
reddening on the topmost bough, far from human hand.
—Was it forgotten in the picking?
— No, not forgotten. It just could not be reached!

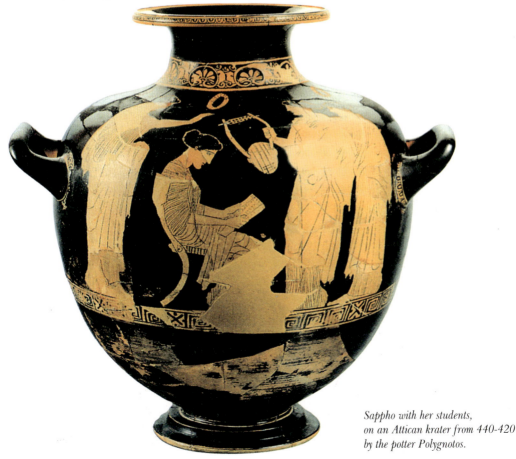

Sappho with her students,
on an Attican krater from 440-420
by the potter Polygnotos.

Anacreon

A lyric poet who was born on the coast of Asia Minor, in the Ionian town of Teo. He lived in the 6th century B.C., left Ionia and went to Avdira, in Thrace where he took part in many battles, events that influenced a number of his poems. The pleasures of the symposiums, to which he refers in other fragments, he learned at the court of Polycrates the lord of Samos. Later he also lived in Athens, a close advisor to the tyrant Ipparchos. His work is written in the Ionian dialect but it contains Aeolian elements from the influence of Sappho and Alcaeus.

Aristippos

Know as the Cyrenaian. He was a Greek philosopher, the founder of the Cyrenaian school. He lived around 435-355 B.C. and originally was a student of Pythagoras. Later he became a student of Socrates and agreed that knowledge had value for a human being only when it fulfilled practical and moral purposes but did not follow the rest of Socrates' philosophical teachings. In his perceptions he identified virtue with sensual pleasure which was attained by sound judgement.

Epicurus

An important Greek philosopher who founded his own philosophical school. He was born on Samos and lived from 341 to 270 B.C. He was an Athenian citizen. Very little has been saved of his large output of writings. According to his philosophy the purpose of life is the enjoyment of the pleasure of the senses, but not ephemeral somatic pleasure; his concept is centered rather on the averting of all bodily pain and psychic disturbance.

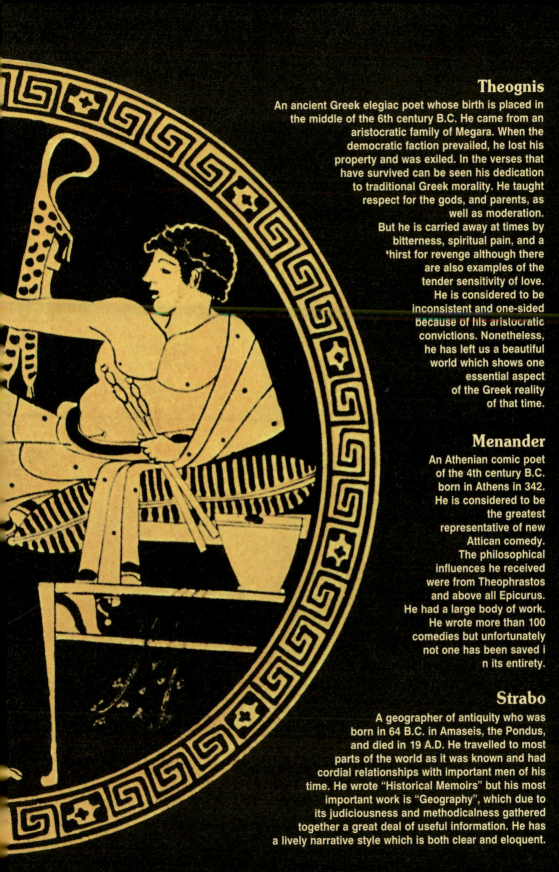

Theognis

An ancient Greek elegiac poet whose birth is placed in the middle of the 6th century B.C. He came from an aristocratic family of Megara. When the democratic faction prevailed, he lost his property and was exiled. In the verses that have survived can be seen his dedication to traditional Greek morality. He taught respect for the gods, and parents, as well as moderation.

But he is carried away at times by bitterness, spiritual pain, and a 'hirst for revenge although there are also examples of the tender sensitivity of love. He is considered to be inconsistent and one-sided because of his aristocratic convictions. Nonetheless, he has left us a beautiful world which shows one essential aspect of the Greek reality of that time.

Menander

An Athenian comic poet of the 4th century B.C. born in Athens in 342. He is considered to be the greatest representative of new Attican comedy. The philosophical influences he received were from Theophrastos and above all Epicurus. He had a large body of work. He wrote more than 100 comedies but unfortunately not one has been saved i n its entirety.

Strabo

A geographer of antiquity who was born in 64 B.C. in Amaseis, the Pondus, and died in 19 A.D. He travelled to most parts of the world as it was known and had cordial relationships with important men of his time. He wrote "Historical Memoirs" but his most important work is "Geography", which due to its judiciousness and methodicalness gathered together a great deal of useful information. He has a lively narrative style which is both clear and eloquent.

In our passage through the ancient Greek world, we paused at those points that are considered to be the most representative periods of cultural achievement, at least in regard to our subject. Perhaps some of you are distressed by the fact that before we arrived at the "practical" matter of love we dealt with theory and a fair dose of philosophy. But we believe that what we are presenting are not points that one can detour around but ones that have to be correctly positioned in both place and time. And again some readers probably have had the thought: "All well and good but what about the simple people, the poor, the uneducated who weren't able to probe into profound meanings, wasn't there any love for them?" And of course there was. They fell in love and perhaps all married for love as well. But unfortunately, it was not the fashion then to write romance novels so there is nothing written concerning that. It is certain, however, that they would have been similar to other romances in every part of the world, and then our interest would not be so focused on classical Greek antiquity. Without neglecting to mention the general social establishment, we have focused most of our attention on those who created the Greek miracle. For the simpler and more reticent, no matter how they functioned within this regime, one thing is certain: they experienced that miracle. The public spaces with the tasteful edifices and the artistic masterpieces were accessible to all. Thanks to democracy they all had access to the marketplace where the orators spoke and the bema ("tribune")where the great male politicians stood. They took part in democratic processes for the election of their archons. So they all lived within this love for the beautiful. But both they and the inspirers of these values would not have been able to imagine that the torch of their inexhaustible wisdom would light the course of humanity right down to the present day.

has remained

If we sought right from the beginning not to fall into the trap of prejudice and prejudgment, which are never productive, it was because whatever weaknesses we happened to note in the ancient Greek world, there was not only no other society at that time to compare to it, but it also had a number of exceedingly strong points that would be still worth promoting today to secure a better life. The ancient thinkers, from Plato to Aristotle, from Epicurus to Plutarch, each left his own distinctive mark on the gradual process of differentiation that eventually created the uniqueness of the ancient world and this process has brought us slowly right up to the present with all the changes and developments that society has gone through. We are living in a period, unfortunately, where an effort is needed to get in touch with these ancient values. But putting aside what has changed, let us look back and consider what has remained:

The ancient Greek Eros (Cupid), did not only flutter playfully above the altars of Aphrodite and the priestesses of love. He also spread his wings in praise of female beauty and the love of woman in the figure of Helen. He gave his illumination to Achilles in order that he might become not only the most beautiful but also the bravest and the noblest of the Achaeans. In rare moments of spiritual fruitfulness this Eros came to be reborn through the theory of Platonic philosophy. Here in Greece, Eros left behind what was cheap and base and became the longing of the soul for eternal beauty and virtue. We are talking of the love that in the union of body with body wants nothing more than immortality through its descendants and in its most spiritual form unites perfect souls which then give birth to healthy institutions and rules for the foundation of life. Yes, this Eros was born here, in Greece. He could have chosen no other country for his homeland than this land which embraces all the divine charms and virtues with everlasting love!

Sophia Souli

Index of the principal names

Bibliograph

Plato, The Symposium
Xenophon, Memoirs, The Symposium, Lacaedamian Republic
Demosthenes, "Against Neairas"
Lucian, Hetairian Dialogues, "Concerning the House".
Athenaeus: "Deipnosophistai, Book II".
Aristophanes, "Clouds".
Plutarch, "Lykourgos", "On Love".
Aeschines, "Against Timarchos"
Theodosios Venizelos, "On The Private Life of the ancient Greeks"
Brouwer, Histoire de la civilisation moral et religeuse des grècs.
K.J. Dover, Greek Homosexuality.
Marion Giebel, Sappho.
P. Darblay, Les hetaires célèbre.
E. Deschanel, Les courtisanes greques.
Dufour, Histoire de la prostitution
Hans Licht, Sexual Life in Ancient Greece.
H.I. Marrou, History of Education in Antiquity.
L. Schmidt, The Ethics of the Ancient Greeks.
Robert Flaceliére, L'amour en Grèce
Robert Flaceliére, La vie quotidienne en Grèce au siècle du Periclés.

Texts: SOPHIA SOULI
Translation of poems and inscriptions from ancient Greek: SOFIA SOULI
Cover page supervision: PANTELIS ASSIMAKOPOULOS
Artistic Editor: NORA ANASTASOGLOU

Production - Printing: M. Toubis S.A.